BASED ON THE HIT amc TV SERIES

THE amc WALKING DEAD

THE OFFICIAL COOKBOOK
AND SURVIVAL GUIDE

BASED ON
THE HIT
aMC
TV SERIES

aMC® THE WALKING DEAD®

THE OFFICIAL COOKBOOK
AND SURVIVAL GUIDE

WRITTEN BY
Lauren Wilson

PHOTOGRAPHY BY
Yunhee Kim

INSIGHT
EDITIONS

San Rafael, California

CONTENTS

KEEP GOING.
ONLY THING HERE
FOR YOU IS TROUBLE.

Introduction

SINCE THE VERY FIRST EPISODE OF AMC'S *THE WALKING DEAD*, the living have fought to stay alive. But as the members of Rick Grimes's group quickly discovered, survival comes in many forms. Sometimes it means risking their lives to fight off countless walkers and create a safe place they can call home. But almost as often, survival simply means finding clean water or a single can of baked beans to warm over a makeshift fire. In a world that tests their limits every day, maintaining physical strength through proper nutrition is paramount . . . something easier said than done.

Generally speaking, people today tend to lack even the most basic survival skills. For characters on *The Walking Dead*, those skills became necessities after the farms and factories ceased their output and the store shelves were picked clean. Their new world left them no other options if they wanted to remain among the living. Fires had to be built. Water had to be boiled. Food had to be foraged and hunted.

In a landscape teeming with walkers, a few simple skills could mean the difference between eating and being eaten. Learning to find water and build a fire are great first steps. After that, one must learn to effectively scavenge abandoned landscapes; forage wild foods; grow one's own fruits and vegetables; and hunt, fish, and preserve any edible bounty they are fortunate enough to accumulate. Within these pages you'll find skills, tips, and tricks Rick and the gang have used to survive, along with how to prepare delicious meals you won't want to wait until the apocalypse to make. You'll find recipes inspired by the characters on the show and their world, a world where electricity is spotty and you never quite know what might be lurking at the bottom of your drinking well, and where you may have to become proficient at squirrel-hunting or buy allegiance with cookies—a world where nothing can be taken for granted and every meal should be savored.

Living or dead, there's one thing that unites us all—hunger.

Chapter I
Food Survival Basics

Even though our world has yet to become infested with wandering hordes of hungry corpses, some survivalists—as well as organizations like the Red Cross and CDC—agree that there are some very basic provisions you can have in place at home, at work, and in your car to help make the transition into any emergency scenario slightly less terrifying.

In the case of Rick and his crew, a few days' worth of supplies would clearly not have been anywhere near enough. None of them could have anticipated how drastically the world would change in such a short time. The following tips should help you avoid being unprepared if the world changes for the worse overnight.

FOR THE HOME

In *The Walking Dead*, it is not uncommon for an entire area to become overwhelmed by walkers with no warning. Something as simple as a loud sound or an enticing smell can draw them in the same direction and create a veritable tidal wave of the dead.

In any situation where you find yourself in danger and unable to flee your home base—or if you should deliberately choose to hunker down and defend your homestead at any cost—you should always have the following minimum supplies on hand:

- One gallon of water per person per day, for drinking and cleaning (minimum three days)
- Nonperishable food, enough for at least two thousand calories per person per day (minimum three days)— freeze-dried, dehydrated, canned, etc.
- An inverter, solar charger, or other power pack (see "Power Hacks" guide)
- Battery-powered or hand-crank radio
- Emergency toilet and sanitation kit
- Walkie-talkies
- Flashlights
- Batteries
- First aid kit
- Manual can opener
- Local maps
- Boards, trip wires, and other supplies to fortify your home

HAVE A GAME PLAN

Even in the real world, not every situation ever ends exactly as planned. For the survivors on *The Walking Dead*, however, staying alive has consistently meant having to think fast and act faster. While just holing up at home may seem like the safest and most logical option in an emergency—undead-related or otherwise— you never know when things will spiral out of control without a moment's notice.

Whether planning for a natural disaster or the end of the world as we know it, it always helps to have a plan in advance. Be aware of your escape routes, including several alternate paths, and have a safe location identified to which you can flee. Ideally, that destination should offer accessibility, security, and ample natural resources.

Have several copies of paper maps at the ready, high-lighting all possible routes in case you become separated from others and need to regroup later. And, if possible, set up *survival caches* along the routes to ensure that you have food and supplies for the trip. Even a long, dangerous journey can become significantly better when you know there are snacks along the way.

BUG-OUT BAGS

Whether you're fleeing your family home or a heavily fortified prison complex under attack by a rival community, having a well-equipped "bug-out bag" (BOB) could well save your life when the time comes to hit the road. Consider stashing these bags in various locations (your home, car, and office) so that you always have one at the ready. Invest in high-quality, lightweight, weatherproof bags that will withstand the demands of a life on the run. As a general rule of thumb, make sure the total weight of the bag (when packed) is no more than one-third your body weight. Otherwise, hauling it around all day will become difficult.

Some useful items to pack in your BOB include:

- Medical kit
- Portable water treatment (filter or tablets)
- Water bottle
- Emergency water pouches (packaged water)
- High-calorie energy bars
- Survival fishing kit
- Snare wire
- Can opener
- Fire ax (doubles as a weapon!)
- Flint and steel
- Stash of tinder in a waterproof container
- Weatherproof matches
- Emergency "space" blanket
- Plastic tarp
- Binoculars
- Compass
- Maps
- Foraging identification guide
- Flashlight
- Fruit and vegetable seeds
- Duct tape
- Paracord
- Toiletries

SURVIVAL CACHES

In a world like the one seen on *The Walking Dead*, everyone is struggling every day to survive. Being robbed on the roadside by a single desperate survivor or forced into an unfair deal by an organized group of thugs like the Saviors could force even the best forager to have to begin again with nothing, so it's always a good idea to have a backup supply that no one else can find, no matter how skimpy. There's a reason that putting all your eggs in one basket is never a good idea. A survival cache is just that—a collection of supplies stashed away for future use. It's essentially an insurance policy in case the supplies you have on hand are lost to fire, theft, or any other worst-case scenario you care to imagine.

Locations

Caches are often buried underground, but they can be set up inside your home or car as well, if you've got secure enough hiding spots. They can also be strategically hidden along your escape route if you have a predetermined end destination. As long as it is in a location where no one else will think to look, your cache should be waiting there untouched when you finally need it.

Containers

The types of containers that you use for your survival caches can vary, depending on how much you want to store, but it is essential that they are durable and 100 percent waterproof, especially if you are burying them underground. Among survivalists, PVC pipes make for popular cache containers. Most camping supply stores carry waterproof boxes in varying sizes as well.

Items

Caches should contain the basics: water, food, and tools. The essential items previously discussed as parts of your basic home preparedness kit and bug-out bags are a great place to start. Customize your cache's contents to suit your own tastes and needs. Avoid foods with short shelf lives, as there's no way to know when you may actually need to break open your cache.

WATER

Humans can generally survive a mere three days without water, so finding it should be your number one priority in survival situations. Under normal circumstances, you will need two to four quarts of water per day for basic survival, and that will only increase should you have to participate in the kind of arduous activities seen in *The Walking Dead*, such as defending a farm from walkers, fleeing a community of cannibals, or scavenging the wasteland to appease Rick's nemesis, Negan.

Always be aware of the common signs of dehydration, including increased thirst, dry mouth, headache, fatigue, dizziness, and infrequent, bright yellow urine. Once you begin to experience these, it's time to replenish your fluids.

Gathering Water

When the days of turning on the tap or stopping by the local convenience store for some bottled water are long gone, survivors will have to rely on other resources to rehydrate.

Rick's group is often seen carrying refillable bottles of water, often relying on wells for water (unless that well contains a bloated, waterlogged walker, of course), along with other natural sources, such as lakes, rivers, streams, and ponds.

Good old-fashioned paper maps are a great tool for locating natural bodies of water, but if a map isn't available, look for lower ground—water naturally drains downhill. Another strategy is to watch wildlife. The presence of small woodland creatures, such as squirrels, raccoons, and birds, is often a sign that there is a viable water source nearby.

You can find water in residential and commercial areas by running the pipes until empty. Use gravity to your advantage and use the faucets closest to ground level. You can also check toilet tanks and water heaters, because they might contain clean drinkable water. Apartment complexes and office towers offer the best chance of finding a large supply. Also, check commercial buildings for outdoor faucets.

Rainwater is another source of water that can be easily collected and stored. You can collect it with buckets, plastic barrels hooked up to gutters and downspouts, or even a tarp rigged up on sticks in a real pinch.

WATER TO AVOID

Signs that water is undrinkable:

- Stagnant (unmoving) water
- Foul smell
- No plant life
- Bubbles, foam, slime
- Milky color
- Undead body parts

Treating Water

You never know what—or who—might be polluting a water source, so any nonbottled water that you find out in the wild must always be treated before drinking. There are several ways you can make water clean and safe to drink. When your source is relatively absent of debris, dirt, and the dead, you can simply boil it for one to three minutes before drinking (or use purification tablets in the absence of fire or electricity). But, more often than not, water gathered from natural sources will be dirty and require filtration. This is where portable filters come in handy, if you can manage to scavenge one. These all-in-one purification systems are popular among campers, hikers, and survivalists, and they can be as small and light as a water bottle. Some are even built into water bottles themselves. Consider adding a filter to your bug-out-bag before disaster strikes.

Storing Water

Dark-colored, food-grade containers are best for keeping out light and minimizing bacteria and algae growth in your water supply. If you have access to chlorine, four to six drops per gallon will make the water safe for long-term storage. Be sure to rotate your water stores by using the oldest water first.

FIRE

Fire-building skills are a must during the apocalypse, and mastering them requires practice and patience. You never know when you might have to whip up a quick signal fire when searching for a missing comrade or roast a rattlesnake for a hungry traveling companion.

Fire Basics

The three basic components for starting a fire are tinder, kindling, and fuel.

Tinder is any light and highly flammable material you can use to get your flames started, something that will catch a spark quickly and easily—shredded paper, dryer lint, cotton balls covered in Vaseline, etc. Tinder should be bone-dry and loosely balled up for ignition, and it should be flammable enough to ignite with a few sparks from a flint and steel.

Kindling is made from slightly sturdier materials than tinder. Think small sticks, rolled-up paper, strips of cardboard—items that will catch easily and are thick and sturdy enough to provide enough flame to catch the fuel.

Fuel is what feeds the fire while it burns, the most traditional of fuels being large pieces of wood. If collecting wood outdoors, look for hardwoods (maple, oak, beech, etc.) rather than softwoods (pine, fir, cedar, spruce). Softwoods tend to burn faster and smokier than hardwoods, and they will give food a rotten flavor. Make sure the wood you are using is dead and dry—using fresh or green wood will create a lot of smoke and may attract unwanted attention.

Preparation

Select a site that is dry and clear of any brush or overhang that might catch fire. If you plan to use the space repeatedly, line the perimeter with rocks for a more official fire pit. Have all your supplies (tinder, kindling, fuel, fire starter) within arm's reach. You don't want to be carrying your smoldering tinder over to the kindling or fuel. Also, keep a means to extinguish the fire nearby—a pile of dirt or a bucket of water or sand.

Unconventional Ways to Create Sparks

- Car battery and jumper cables

- 9-volt battery and steel wool

- Gunpowder from a bullet

Architecture

Once you know how to get your fire started, the next consideration is how to put the pieces together. No matter how you build your fire, you need to allow space for airflow—otherwise your fire will burn out.

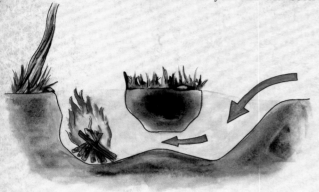

Building your fire in a hole in the ground that connects to a secondary tunnel for airflow—known as a Dakota Fire Hole—is great for concealing your location.

A larger log cabin–style fire can accommodate a suspended pot above it for cooking. A piece of wire mesh over the fire can be used to roast small animals or, if things go terribly wrong, the occasional tainted leg.

For a quick meal, you can build a small kindling fire between two large logs and rest a cooking pot on them.

And if you're caught in the woods with no ax, you can arrange large tree limbs in a star formation and then push them in toward the center of the fire as they burn down.

POWER HACKS

Electricity powers stoves, ovens, refrigerators, and all the other kitchen appliances we take for granted on a day-to-day basis. When the power grid is down, a gasoline-powered generator seems like the most viable solution. Sure, it's perfect for weathering a hurricane, but gasoline is not a reliable resource in an end-of-days scenario. Fortunately, there are alternatives for generating and storing power.

Gasoline

When the pumps run dry and production stops, survivors will have to procure the planet's remaining gasoline supply. While T-Dog may have been a pro at siphoning gasoline out of the tanks of abandoned cars, the yield was low and the taste was horrible. One might be better off searching for larger storage stations, called fuel batteries, where high quantities of gasoline are stored for commercial use.

Something to keep in mind with any gasoline that you might be able to scavenge: Like food, gas has a limited shelf life. Depending on the temperature and other conditions of its storage, gasoline can become useless in a matter of just a few months. You can extend the life of gasoline with gas additives, an option that can be especially useful if you want to stockpile some for your group's caravan of vehicles before a long trip. Additives can extend the life of the fuel for up to eighteen months. In general, diesel fuel lasts two to three times longer than gasoline, and with additives it can be useful for up to ten years. You can find additives at most gas stations and any hardware store, and most folks will be too busy hunting for food or ammo to grab something this practical.

12-Volt Batteries

Another widely available and easily scavenged emergency power source are the 12-volt batteries found in most cars. By connecting these batteries to a *power inverter*—which converts a battery's DC power into AC power—you can then plug in lamps, space heaters, and even some appliances (depending on their wattage).

Most 12-volt car batteries shouldn't be drained to less than 50 percent power or they will suffer lasting damage. Deep-cycle batteries (like marine batteries) are designed to be drained and recharged over and over and are a better long-term solution, so it might be worth a trip to the marina to pick clean some boats.

Power packs are all-in-one solutions that provide a weatherproof housing for the battery, an on-board inverter, 12-volt sockets, AC outlets, USB outlets, and a charger. Certain models can even be hooked up to solar panels. You can buy these ready-made or build one yourself.

Solar Power

The Alexandria Safe-Zone is outfitted with solar panels. In a prolonged survival situation, you might be able to put together a similar configuration to power individual houses or even a whole community. There are ample resources online for assembling your own solar array that are best perused before the Internet is no longer accessible, but the basic components are:

- Solar panels, to form the array
- Inverter, to convert DC power into AC power
- Photovoltaic disconnect, to turn off the power so you can perform maintenance
- Breaker box, where the system connects to the home

Solar panels may not be as abundant or easily attainable as gas or batteries, but for a long-term power solution, there are few better options.

Propane

Commonly used for barbecues and camp lanterns, propane is actually a very versatile fuel and is often found in backcountry locations where power and gas lines do not reach. There are propane-powered versions of virtually every major home appliance—from fridges to washing machines and from water heaters to ranges for cooking. Propane will probably not be as sought after as gasoline, making it a good scavengeable item for your long-term survival community.

SHELF-STABLE FOODS

Most of the fresh foods you've come to depend upon in our preapocalypse world—from fruits and veggies to milk and eggs—are also available in canned, jarred, dehydrated, freeze-dried, or powdered forms. If you want to keep your pantry as well-stocked as Olivia's in Alexandria before the arrival of Negan, it's important to fully understand the benefits and limitations of these different forms of preservation.

Dehydrated

Dehydrated foods have had nearly all (90 to 95 percent) their moisture content removed. They tend to be small, shriveled, and either chewy or hard. These include familiar foods such as jerky, raisins, dates, and figs. You can even purchase a home dehydrator and build your own stash of foods. Pretty much anything—meat, dairy, fruits, and vegetables alike—can be dehydrated and stored for far longer than their original fresh counterparts.

Freeze-dried

Freeze-dried foods have had virtually all (95 to 98 percent) their water content removed. They undergo a different process than dehydrated foods, leaving them lighter and more intact. They are much easier to reconstitute, too, and unlike many dehydrated foods, they don't require cooking. On top of that, the average shelf life of freeze-dried foods is significantly longer: Stored at temperatures of 60°F or below, they can last for twenty-five to thirty years. However, once you open a container of freeze-dried food, you must consume it all quickly, which isn't the case for their dehydrated cousins. You can find freeze-dried meats, cheeses, eggs, fruits, vegetables, and even ice cream at various survival supply outlets (see Resources).

Powdered

Powdered foods undergo a process similar to freeze-drying, but the final product is in powdered form. You can get peanut butter, margarine, butter, whole eggs, egg whites, cheese, sour cream, cream cheese, and buttermilk in powdered form. These products work particularly well as substitutes for fresh ingredients in baking. Be aware, though, that powdered eggs and dairy generally have shorter shelf lives (one to ten years, depending on the product) than other freeze-dried counterparts.

Surprising Things That Come in a Can

Whether you're a hungry survivor scavenging the wasteland or simply an adventurous eater, you might want to keep an eye out for these unusual canned foods to keep things interesting:

- Bread
- Butter
- Cheese
- Peanut butter and jelly sandwiches
- Hamburgers
- Bacon

- Whole chicken
- Alligator
- Rattlesnake
- 112 ounces of chocolate pudding (just ask Carl Grimes!)

SCAVENGING

Scouring a region for food, medicine, and other supplies is no easy task. Once you've depleted the supplies in your immediate surroundings, you will be forced to head farther and farther out from your home base in search of goods.

Forget going to your local big box store, hospital, or gun shop. Those are the places where everyone else will have already scored big (or been devoured whole). Instead, try to think outside the box and scavenge for food and supplies in unlikely locations, such as jails, schools, companies large enough to have employee cafeterias, hardware stores, and even veterinary hospitals.

Strategy

Before you decide to scavenge, you should have a solid plan in place: who's going, what their role will be, what buildings you will target, what to do in case of emergency, and where to meet if things go bad. If we've learned anything from Rick's crew, it's that things can *always* go wrong.

Scavenging can be dangerous. It involves heading into unknown locales, where you are often unsure of what might be lurking around the corner or directly beneath your feet. It is always wise to scavenge with at least one other person, because even if you're unlikely to plunge into a putrid pit of waterlogged walkers, it's still good to know that someone is watching your back.

It should go without saying: scavenge during daylight hours. If you're tackling a large area, like a neighborhood or a city block, break it down into quadrants and tackle them one at a time. Before entering any building, survey the surroundings and exterior, looking for all possible entrances and exits. Always try to assess whether anyone—living or dead—might be inside before entering.

When searching a space for useful items, be thorough. Check in drawers, under mattresses, in closets, in garages, etc. Have a notepad so you can jot down locations and items you might need to come back for. Be creative! Most everyday items can take on second lives—empty soda bottles can be used to grow food, steel drums can be used for makeshift ovens, and the wire from picture frames can be used as hunting snares.

When you leave a locale, consider marking all buildings you have emptied with spray paint or some kind of sign—from a simple X to a practical message, such as EMPTY—so that you don't accidentally waste time retracing your steps. If you have a paper map, mark down all territory you've covered.

Supplies

These are some basic tools and supplies that will make scavenging that much easier:

- Bolt cutters
- Crowbar
- Lock-pick kit
- Flashlight
- Bags: backpacks, duffel bags, etc.
- Protective gear
- Paper map to mark off completed areas

Canned Foods to Avoid When Scavenging

Many canned foods can be eaten safely well past their "best before" date, unless they've been spoiled by damage or improper storage. These dates are meant as a general recommendation for avoiding spoilage, but there are some telltale signs that will let you know if a canned item is no longer good to eat:

- Bulging sides, top, or bottom
- Deep dents near the top, bottom, or seams
- Leaking of any kind
- Rust/corrosion of any kind
- Food popping out or exploding when opened
- Foul smell inside
- Unusual bubbles or foaming inside

BARTERING

Aside from meeting your own needs, scavenging could also be a great way to amass goods for bartering. A barter-based economy may become the norm if our traditional economy collapses, and knowing which items would be most valuable could go a long way in getting yourself or your community the supplies you need.

At its most basic, bartering consists of trading goods or services without the use of money—such as Alexandria providing protection to the Hilltop community in exchange for supplies. Bartering can become infinitely more complex when you bring in additional parties for multiway trades or if the items being traded are a combination of various goods and services.

Unless you know and trust your bartering partners, be cautious when exchanging information about what you have to barter. Not tipping your hand could save you from being robbed.

Valuable Items to Barter

- Toiletries such as toilet paper, feminine products, diapers, toothpaste, soap
- Fuel of all kinds
- Alcohol
- Over-the-counter drugs like pain relievers and cold medicines
- Batteries of all types
- Solar chargers
- Cigarettes
- Potable water

FORAGING

Whether trekking through the back roads of Georgia or hunkering down in the suburbs of Washington, DC, you can generally find edible wild foods in fields, backyards, and parks anywhere. The following are some tried-and-true methods for determining whether a wild food is edible.

Universal Edibility Test

This is a slow and methodical method to safely determine whether a plant is edible. First, break down the plant into its various parts—flowers, leaves, stem, root, etc. Then, lightly bruise one part of the specimen and rub it on the inside of your elbow. Hold it there for fifteen minutes. If no reaction occurs, touch a small piece of the bruised specimen to your lips for five minutes. If no burning, itching, or other reaction occurs, hold a piece on your tongue for three minutes. Now, chew the specimen and hold it in your mouth. If it tastes bitter or soapy, spit it out. If there is no negative reaction after fifteen minutes, swallow the specimen and wait for eight

hours. If no vomiting or diarrhea develops, eat a small handful and wait another eight hours. If no reaction occurs, this part of the plant is safe to eat. Hopefully, it tastes good enough to be worth all the hassle you've gone through to get to this point.

Plants to Avoid

The universal edibility test is a great way to definitively tests plants for safety, but there are some general characteristics that signal plants to avoid:

- Spines, fine hairs, or thorns
- Sap that is milky or discolored
- Foliage that looks like dill, carrot, or parsley
- Almondlike scent in the woody parts and leaves of a plant
- Grain heads with pink, purplish, or black spurs

A Note About Mushrooms

While foraging for mushrooms might sound like a fun postapocalyptic escape, there are far too many poisonous look-alikes for it to be worthwhile unless you have a colored foraging guide or experienced forager in your group.

QUICK-AND-DIRTY GROWING GUIDE

Should the day come when your local grocery store has been cleaned out, the only way you're likely to see another fresh vegetable in your lifetime is if you grow it yourself. Of course, as Hershel Greene's family learned all too well in Season 2, a working farm isn't always an option for long-term living. Even if you don't have a patch of land to cultivate, a green thumb can still be put to great use in a cold, gray world.

The Importance of Seeds

You can't grow anything without seeds. While you can collect seeds from foraged fruits and vegetables, your best bet will be to store seeds ahead of time, then replenish your stock from your new plants. Some sellers even offer "survival seed vaults" that have a variety of seeds for your postapocalyptic growing needs. Many of these vaults contain only "crop year seeds," which are intended for use in the same year that they're packaged due to their relatively high moisture content. Seeds that have been properly dried for long-term storage tend to be more expensive but are worth the investment.

If you didn't plan ahead, try scavenging for seeds in home and garden or hardware stores, backyard sheds, community gardens, and local farms.

Container Growing

Throughout the world of *The Walking Dead*—from the prison yard and Terminus to the Hilltop and the Kingdom communities—container growing has proven to be a versatile method of raising crops.

You can be pretty inventive when it comes to the types of containers you use as growing vessels. While existing pots and planters were designed for the job, coffee tins, bathtubs, and rubber boots can do just as well in a pinch. Just be sure to collect containers with a variety of widths and depths, as different root systems have different needs. Puncture the bottoms of any unconventional vessels to allow for proper drainage.

Also, try to avoid any containers that might have a varnish or finish that could leach into the soil or might have previously housed poisonous or otherwise harmful contents. If the container needs to stay outside, make sure it is weather resistant.

Potting Soil

More important than the container itself is the soil that you use. Because container plants are housed in a confined space, they need a soil that will allow for quick and easy drainage. In the absence of commercial potting soils, you can concoct your own mixture using one half earth, one quarter coarse sand, one eighth sawdust, one eighth finely shredded newspaper, and a sprinkling of broken-up charcoal (burnt wood from a fire also works fine).

Watering and Drainage

Container plants tend to dry out quicker than plants in the ground and will require more frequent watering, so check often until you become acquainted with the plants' needs. Your plants will need proper drainage when housed in containers, so make sure to add holes to the bottom of any nonconventional vessels you might be using. You will know there is proper drainage when the water flows through easily and steadily after watering. Elevate your containers so that they can drain freely. And be sure to pay close attention, as overwatered plants can display similar symptoms to those that are underwatered.

Feeding Your Plants

Container plants will also run out of nutrients quicker than plants in the ground, requiring you to provide additional nutrition. In general, plants need three main nutrients: nitrogen, hydrogen, and potassium. They also need sulfur, calcium, and magnesium in small quantities. Compost is a great source of all-around nutrition if available. Pine needles, coffee grounds, ashes from wood fires, and even urine can offer additional nutrients, but those tend to alter the soil's pH level, so use sparingly.

Indoor Growing

Indoor growing will more often than not mean low-light growing. If you're growing anywhere with limited direct sunlight (and this applies to some outdoor gardens as well), you will need plants that can manage with less light:

• Leafy greens like kale, chard, lettuce, spinach, and arugula

• Bush varieties of peas and beans

• Roots and tubers like potatoes, carrots, beets, and radishes

• Herbs like chives, parsley, bay leaves, and mint

Some vegetables—such as romaine, scallions, bok choy, and celery—are even able to regrow themselves when their root ends are submerged in water and exposed to light.

Rooftop Growing

As witnessed at Grady Memorial Hospital in Season 5, rooftop farming can offer many of the benefits of growing in the ground—full sun most crucially—without the hassle of having to erect walls and fences to keep predators out. All the plants you can grow in low-light conditions can also be grown on a rooftop and shaded as needed. You can also grow fruiting plants like squash, tomato, cucumber, eggplant, and berries. Be sure to have barriers on hand to protect your plants from wind and sun as needed. And be conscious of the size of your rooftop farm, because soil and containers are heavy (especially when soil is wet), and too much weight could cause the roof to collapse.

Protecting Your Bounty

Unless you are growing your plants on a rooftop, constructing fencing around the entirety of your garden is a good idea to keep out humans, animals, and any other unwanted guests. If deer are an issue, you will need these fences to be at least eight feet tall. You will also want to root the fence two to three feet underground to keep out pests like rabbits, who can burrow under shallow fences.

Humans are a little harder to keep out—and we're not just talking about the undead variety. Tall fences that are padlocked can be effective, as can spiky and stinging plants in the garden. And you can always fortify the perimeter of your garden with a DIY security system. Simple booby traps and sharp wooden spikes can go a long way to keep people from invading your space. Just ask Morgan.

HUNTING BASICS

Hunting skills will come in handy during postapocalypse times—and not just for making a fashionable sash of squirrel pelts like the one worn by Daryl Dixon. Even if you never have a chance to go hunting before the world ends, this guide will give you the basics for finding, hunting, and trapping your next meal.

Tracking

The first step in hunting your dinner is finding it, and that means tracking. Tracking requires a keen eye—you need to pick up subtle signs that under normal circumstances you'd probably overlook. Most animals live close to a water source, so start there and work your way out. Many animals will also habitually use the same paths to go between their den and the water source, so look for a well-worn trail. These could be good places to set snares or hunker down before dawn and wait. The majority of animals are generally most active in the first and last hours of sunlight, so those are good times to observe and hunt.

Hunting

Animals are well equipped to sense our presence. The human form, our faces, and our hands are very recognizable to wild animals, which is why hunters go to great lengths to cover up and blend into their surroundings with camouflage. If you can't scavenge camouflage gear, choose neutral colors that will blend into your surroundings.

Our smell is also very recognizable, so try to stay downwind when possible and wear clean clothing that has been saturated with smoke from a fire. To avoid detection, you must also be extremely quiet, moving very consciously and slowly through brush.

Planting is one approach to hunting, where you stay in one very well-concealed spot and wait for your prey. This is a great choice when you know where your prey dens.

Stalking means following your prey until you have a clear shot. It requires stealth and practice, but it is an effective method for hunting moose, deer, and elk, among others.

Flushing and driving means walking through an area to flush out animals from hiding in the brush, bushes, and trees. This technique is best done in pairs, where one can flush and the other can shoot. It's a great method for hunting small prey like rabbits, raccoons, opossums, pheasants, and grouse.

Trapping

Trapping is a good option when you don't have a gun or crossbow. Traps are also beneficial because you can set them and leave them while you focus on more important things—like trying to defend your colony from bloodthirsty rival gangs. There are many ways to trap animals, some of them quite complex and tailored to specific species. The noose snare is a basic tool to help you get started.

Noose Snare

As Rick explained to Carl and Michonne while they were traveling to Terminus in Season 4, this classic beginner's trap is quite easy to set, requiring nothing more than snare wire and a stick. It's a good trap to use on trails and well-worn paths that animals use habitually.

Once an animal walks through the snare, the noose will tighten around its neck. You will need to attach the noose to a low-hanging branch or sturdy stake, making sure the stake is plunged deep enough into the ground to withstand the animal's movement. Be sure to position the stake so that the noose is at neck height of the intended prey.

When setting up snares, avoid using your bare hands because they'll leave a strong scent that will scare off prey. If you must use your bare hands, try running the snare quickly through some flames to remove your odor.

NOTE: Basic snares are generally illegal in our pre-apocalyptic world, so until the walkers take over, be sure to consult your local fish and wildlife agency for the hunting rules and regulations governing your area.

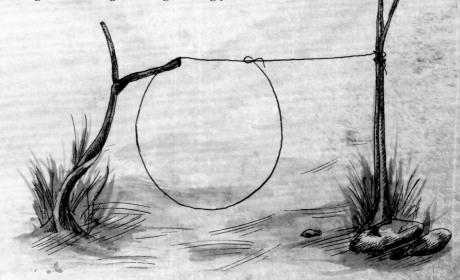

COMMON FISH AND WILD GAME

This is a general overview of the game used in recipes throughout this book, along with tips and tricks for tracking them down. Wild game varies by region, so be sure to consult local guides and hunting regulations before venturing out. For more detailed hunting information, check out the Further Reading section.

Panfish

Varieties: Bluegill, Crappies, Spotted Bass, Yellow Perch

Difficulty: Easy

Where to Hunt Them: Freshwater lakes and streams, near sunken logs, boulders, boats, in shade, in coves

Hunting Tips: Use small hooks that aren't shiny. For bluegills, try crickets or worms as bait; for crappies and yellow perch, try live minnows; for bass, try worms. These panfish can be fished in winter.

Culinary Notes: This class of fish is called "panfish" because they are generally small enough to fit right in the pan. Season liberally as they can be bland.

Opossum and Raccoon

Difficulty: Moderate

Where to Hunt Them: Varied habitat in urban, suburban, and wilderness settings

Hunting Tips: Look for their distinctive humanlike paw prints and hunt at night. Snares and traps can also be used.

Culinary Notes: These are known scavengers and carrion (dead animal) eaters, so if you can trap them and feed them a vegetable diet before dispatching, they will make for a better meal.

Grouse and Pheasant

Difficulty: Moderate to hard, depending on region

Where to Hunt Them: Often found close to grain farmland; they tend to forage on the forest floor, typically in some form of cover.

Hunting Tips: These woodland birds are often hunted with dogs using a flushing and driving technique, but it can be done without them. Snares and traps can also be effective.

Culinary Notes: Depending on their diet and habitat, these birds can be quite delicious. Roasting them with the skin on is a classic way to prepare them.

Rabbit

Difficulty: Moderate to hard

Where to Hunt Them: Brush, bramble, open woodlots, edge habitats

Hunting Tips: Look for bushes, brush piles, or any other habitat offering dense cover. A method often used is "walking up," which entails walking through the rabbits' known habitats to cause them to bolt. Snares and traps are also effective. When using a gun, aim at the head to avoid damaging the meat; you want the back legs intact, as that is where most of the meat is!

Culinary Notes: Because rabbit is so lean, it can cause a condition of fat starvation called "rabbit starvation" if eaten in excess. Their leanness also makes it difficult to cook them whole without braising. They can also carry a disease called tularemia, so wear gloves when butchering, and discard if the animal appears sickly. The meat is delicious in stews (see Simple Herb-Braised Rabbit).

When to Eat Rattlesnake

The answer is . . . when you haven't eaten for days and Daryl roasts it whole, then tosses a segment of it your way. Actually, if you do ever catch a rattlesnake for dinner, be sure to remove its head with extreme caution, as you can still be bitten and injected with venom even after the snake is dead. Get the head off and discard it without physically handling it in any way. And before you roast it whole à la Daryl Dixon, be sure to skin and remove the guts first! The skin can be peeled off like a very tight stocking.

Squirrel

Difficulty: Moderate (urban) to hard (forest dwelling)

Where to Hunt Them: Woodlands, parks, other green spaces

Hunting Tips: It's true; squirrels love nuts, so look for nut-bearing trees. Because squirrels can be so skittish, planting near a known den is an effective method. They tend to hide high up in trees, so you may need to make some noise to scare them out (but take care not to attract walkers). Remove the hide while the squirrels are still warm.

Culinary Notes: Squirrels don't have a lot of meat, and it will likely be tough. Braising is a great option (see Squirrel Piquante). Their flavor is generally mild.

Why Squirrel Tartare Isn't a Good Idea

Remember when Daryl was impaled with one of his own arrows and then started to hallucinate a pep talk from Merle? Well, he also had a creek-side dinner of squirrel tartare, and, in that dire survival situation, it probably saved his life. But squirrels are known to carry the disease tularemia, so always cook them thoroughly.

Counting Calories During the Apocalypse

Did you know that if Michonne was to swing her katana for an hour she would burn approximately four hundred to six hundred calories? Though you may have counted your own calories before to avoid consuming *too many*, in the event of a walker apocalypse you'd need to start counting them to make sure you were getting *enough*. Calories would be hard to come by, so most dietary restrictions and personal preferences would have to be thrown out the window. On top of that, the days of being sedentary would be over. The average active survivor on *The Walking Dead*——whether running around evading walkers, shoring up defenses on the wall, or farming vegetables——would likely need about three thousand calories per day, a full thousand more than the average person does now.

Whitetail Deer

Difficulty: Moderate to hard, depending on location and population density

Where to Hunt Them: Habitat varies greatly with geography, but generally woodlands with ample hiding places

Hunting Tips: Deer generally have a home range of about a half square mile and are intimately familiar with this area. Their sense of smell is legendary, so it is best to take precautions such as smoking your clothing and staying downwind. Look for tracks and droppings.

Culinary Notes: Deer provide a whole lot of meat. Consider drying extra meat into jerky (see DIY Deer Jerky) or a delicious stew (see Dixon Deer Stew). Flavor will vary drastically depending on geography and the deer's diets. Definitely do not eat a deer if a walker has gotten their paws on it!

FISHING BASICS

You may not have spent your entire childhood in a boat like Andrea and Amy, but that doesn't mean you can't net a major haul of fish and be the hero of your survival group. In a dire situation, you can rig up a fishing pole using nothing but some line, a modified soda can tab, and a stick.

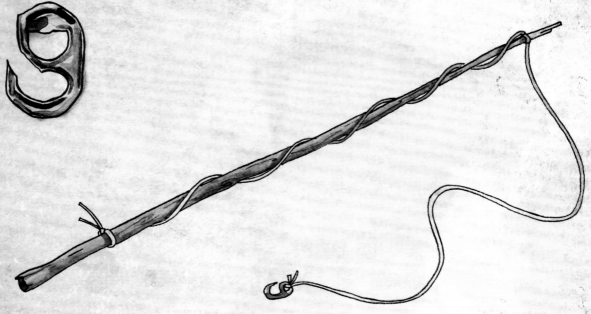

Knots

Fishing is also a chance to practice another important survival skill—tying knots. In Season 1, Amy swore her dad tied only fisherman's or clinch knots, while Andrea swore it was nail knots. Either way, there are lots of knots to be learned for a wide range of situations. The good news is, you can get by with one simple and highly versatile knot—the improved clinch knot. It can be used to attach your line to your pole, and your hook to your line, along with any number of other uses. Plus, it's quick and easy to learn as well as to tie (see right).

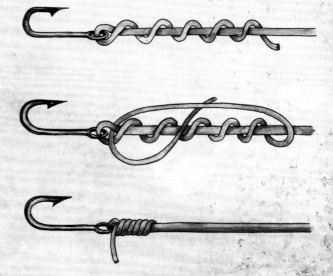

Set Lines

Once you've got a pole rigged up, you're ready to fish. When you've got a dangerous world to navigate and don't have the time to stay in one place, you can *set your line*. Plant it firmly in the bank (far enough back so that it's secure), cast the line, and let nature take its course. If you can bait your hook first, even better.

Bait

Thoughts of fishing may conjure images of an earthworm wriggling on the end of your hook, but modern anglers prefer synthetic forms of bait, called flies and lures. These require less effort to acquire, are reusable, and won't stink up your fridge.

Using live bait requires a little more effort in the absence of bait shops, since you'll have to catch the bait yourself. But if you can't scavenge some synthetic lures, then old-fashioned bait like earthworms, minnows, and crickets will do just fine.

Scaling and Cleaning Fish

Fish spoil fast, so keep them alive and in water until you're ready to clean and cook them. Cleaning fish can be surprisingly messy, so it's usually a good idea to do it outside. Wear rubber gloves if you have them, and always sharpen your knife before you begin.

Scaling

1. Rinse off the fish thoroughly and pat it dry. Lay the fish on its side, with the head covered by your nondominant hand.
2. Using a small sharp knife, work from the tail toward the head in short, quick strokes. Don't push too hard or you will damage the meat (or your hand)!
3. When done, rinse the fish again and pat dry. Check to make sure the fish is smooth all over.

Gutting

1. Lay the fish on its side, with the head covered by your nondominant hand and the belly facing you. Starting at the anus, make a shallow incision through the center of the belly up to the base of the gills. Too deep a cut will nick the innards.
2. Open up the belly and remove the entrails. Rinse out the inside of the fish thoroughly.

Filleting

1. Holding the head in your dominant hand with the belly facing you, cut off the tail and fins.
2. Working through the gills, cut off the head, then turn your knife so that the blade faces the tail.
3. Slip your knife into the fish at a 45-degree angle, and get as close to the rib cage as you can. Use it as a guide and cut with a smooth sweeping motion down to the tail. Remove the fillet.
4. Repeat on the other side.

Skinning

1. Lay your fillet skin side down, with the tail end on your dominant hand's side.
2. Starting at the tail end, slip your knife under the skin as close to it as possible. Trim a little away, then grab the skin and hold it as you trim the rest using short, smooth strokes.
3. Repeat for the other fillet.

FOOD PRESERVATION

Hopefully, your container garden is so productive that you've grown more baby beets than you can consume. Or perhaps you're hunting so well that you now rival Daryl himself in your ability to put a steaming hot bowl of Squirrel Piquante on the table. If you're fortunate enough to have an excess of anything during the apocalypse (and you don't have to pony up half of it to Negan), then it may be time to master the all-important skill of preservation. Food preservation can take many forms, including canning, fermenting, drying, smoking, and curing. All of them can be extremely useful for when your times of feast inevitably turn to famine.

Canning

Hot-water canning is a way of preserving foods by sealing them in a clean, airtight container and "processing" them in a hot-water bath to pasteurize them for long-term storage. It does require some specialized equipment, like mason jars, threaded bands, and self-sealing lids. Luckily, these should be relatively easy to scavenge, and since they are made in standard sizes, most brands will fit together seamlessly.

How to Hot-Water Can

1. In your canning pot, boil all the equipment that will come in direct contact with the food *except for the lids.* (Boiling the lids can damage them and cause an improper seal.) Boil for ten minutes to sterilize. Turn down the heat, add the lids, and keep on a gentle simmer until you are ready to use them.

2. When your recipe is ready, remove the jars, bands, and lids from the pot and shake off as much excess water as you can. Fill the warm jar with your recipe, leaving the "headspace" (empty space at the top of the jar) specified in your recipe—it's usually one-quarter inch to one-half inch. Stir the contents to release any lingering air bubbles, and wipe the rim clean if necessary. Put on the lid and band.

3. Put the jars back into the pot, and add more water if needed—the jars should be covered by at least an inch of water. Bring it back to a boil. This is when you begin the "processing time." Boil for the time specified in your recipe, often fifteen to twenty minutes. Remove the pot from the heat and let it sit for five minutes before transferring the jars to a sturdy surface to cool completely over twenty-four hours. You should hear the jars popping periodically; this means they are sealing.

4. After twenty-four hours, remove the screw bands and check that the lids are adhering tightly to the jar. Replace the bands and store your jars in a cool, dark place.

Pickling

Pickling is a very popular way of preserving food using the aforementioned canning method. We all know that Rick has a penchant for cucumber farming, but you can pickle far more than the traditional cucumber—including hot peppers (see The Governor's Pickled Peppers) and eggs (see Carriage Bar Pickled Eggs).

The main ingredient in any canned pickle recipe, aside from the food itself, is the brine. Brine refers to the vinegar-and-salt-based solution that you submerge the food in. Traditional pickling add-ins include sugar, garlic cloves, fresh herbs, peppercorns, mustard seeds, and chile flakes. Make sure your brine is hot when adding it to the jars, to encourage better penetration. Blanch especially crunchy vegetables (like beets) before canning so that they will soften enough to be enjoyable.

Jamming

Jamming is another favorite preservation method. Jam's spreadable texture is the result of three main ingredients: pectin, acid, and sugar. There are commercially produced powdered versions of both pectin and citric acid available, but these chemical components also occur naturally in most fruits. If you can't scavenge pectin or citric acid, you can combine fruits to achieve the same results (see the following list). Slightly underripe fruits will have the highest acid and pectin content and are often used in jamming for this reason.

Sugar is the last component of jamming, and it is key in creating the jam's unique consistency. It also acts as a preservative that deters the growth of certain bacteria and molds. Plus, if you are using underripe fruits for their pectin and acid, you will need the sugar for extra flavor. The general rule of thumb for jam-making is a 1:1 fruit-to-sugar ratio.

Pectin and Acid in Fruit

High pectin: Sweet oranges, tangerines, sweet apples

High acid: Apricots, pomegranates, strawberries, sour cherries, pineapples, raspberries, rhubarb

High acid and high pectin: Tart apples, cranberries, blackberries, gooseberries, lemons, red currants, grapes

Fermenting

Humans have been fermenting foods for thousands of years. It's a tried and true way of preserving foods that is remarkably easy. On a microscopic level, fermenting is technically the transformation of foods by microorganisms— lactic acid bacteria, to be exact—while imbuing them with natural preservatives. Lactic acid bacteria also predigests foods for us, making the nutrients easier to absorb while also releasing new nutrients. Popular fermented products include sauerkraut, kimchi, vinegar, and beer.

While you might need to scavenge some basics, such as salt, fermentation doesn't require much in the way of specialized equipment. You can ferment in most food-safe noncorrosive containers, like jars and ceramic crocks. Narrow-necked vessels are great for making alcoholic beverages, such as Honey Mead, because they minimize the liquid's exposure to oxygen. Wide-mouthed vessels allow for maximum oxygenation, so they are great for making vinegars.

You can ferment virtually any vegetable, though some end up much tastier than others. Vegetables with a high water content (like zucchini or bell peppers) tend to become overly mushy, while dense and crunchy veggies (like cabbage, broccoli, carrots, beets, and radishes) ferment quite well. Salt is used in vegetable fermentation both for flavor and to give certain beneficial microbes a competitive advantage.

Surface mold and foam are often natural parts of the fermentation process and can be skimmed off with no ill effects. But if your fermented food has a foul or putrid smell, a deeply penetrating mold, or a slimy consistency, it may be unsafe to eat.

Air-Drying Fruits and Vegetables

In the right weather and climate, air-drying foods is easy. The community at Grady Memorial Hospital had a great rooftop setup where they needed nothing more than the breeze and sunshine to preserve fresh fruits and vegetables for later use.

Temperatures of at least 85°F are ideal, but you also need relatively low humidity (60 percent or lower). Long periods with no rain are also required, since air-drying takes several days (three to seven for most fruits and vegetables). This makes the method impractical in some regions and seasons, though the residents at Grady still managed to make it work even in Atlanta's humid climate.

Air-drying can be used on nearly any fruit, vegetable, or meat. Fruits are the safest for beginners, though, because their high sugar and acid contents help to prevent spoilage while drying. Foods should be peeled, seeded, and cut into thin uniform pieces so that they dry at the same pace. Foods that tend to oxidize and turn brown (like apples) should be tossed in lemon juice.

Because drying racks must provide unobstructed airflow, the surface you lay the food on needs to be very porous, such as a stainless steel mesh or cheesecloth stretched over a wooden frame. Once lined with food for drying, the trays should be situated in a place that gets direct sunlight and a good breeze. Cover the trays with additional netting or cheesecloth to keep off dust and pests. Turn the food once per day and, if necessary, move the tray around to keep it in direct sunlight. Bring the food indoors at night to keep it safe from animals and prevent moisture from seeping back in.

If you have access to an oven, heat the food at about 175°F for thirty minutes to kill off any insects or their eggs once the food is done drying. Before you can store your dried foods, you need to condition them to redistribute any remaining moisture evenly throughout the batch. Put the dried food into a large plastic or glass container and seal it shut. Shake it daily for seven to ten days, examining it daily for signs of spoilage. Store the dried foods in clean, tightly sealed containers and keep them in a cool, dark place. The cooler the temperature, the longer the food will last.

PRESERVING MEAT

Drying

Like fruit, meat can also be sun- and air-dried, but there is certainly more room for error. If the climate is not dry or cool enough, the meat will spoil before it dries. When an oven is not available, sunny, windy, and cold climates are best for drying meat. You can tell that the meat has sufficiently dried if it cracks when you bend it.

Dried meats can sometimes be reconstituted in recipes, such as Alexandria resident Spencer Monroe's infamous beef jerky stroganoff. Though the meat's texture might not be quite the same after it has been dried, the flavors remain mostly intact.

Smoking

Smoking is another way to dry meat, one that uses the antimicrobial properties of smoke to protect the meat while also giving it an intense flavor boost. Smoke also slows the oxidization of fat in the meat, which is what causes dried meats to become rancid. Be sure to trim all fat off your meat before drying or smoking. Use only hardwoods as softwoods like pines, firs, and other coniferous trees will make the meat taste awful. See Building a Smoke Tepee for more detail.

Salting (aka Dry Curing)

Dry curing is a preservation method where salt is applied directly to the meat to draw out moisture and inhibit harmful bacteria and enzymes. Sugar and other seasonings can also be used for flavor. Salting is best done in cool and dry climates and seasons, where temperatures are 50°F or cooler and the humidity is in the 60 to 65 percent range. As a rule of thumb, use 6 percent salt by weight of the meat.

For a short cure, you can cover the meat in salt and put into a nonreactive pan or dish, covering it well to keep out pests. Store it below 50°F, draining and flipping it every few days until the meat has lost 15 percent of its weight (about two days per pound). Rinse off the salt, and cook it before eating.

To fully cure the meat: After the initial salting described above, cover the meat with a layer of lard and several layers of cheesecloth. Hang it to age in a cool place for about six months, or until it has lost 30 percent of its original weight. Fully cured salted meats do not need to be cooked. They will be quite salty and are best enjoyed thinly sliced or used sparingly in soups. You can also soak them to remove some of the salt, as is often done with salt cod.

COOKING AND BAKING WITH FIRE

While the recipes in this book provide directions for traditional cooking methods, most can be adapted for cooking over a fire. It's a good idea to practice cooking a few meals outdoors with no electricity to hone your skills. As seen on *The Walking Dead*, a postapocalyptic scenario can force you to rely on your survival capabilities. When cooking with fire, follow these basic practices for best results.

Cooking Tips

In general, use live flames for general cooking, such as frying, sautéing, and braising. Try to find dry, dead hardwoods (e.g. maple, oak, and birch). "Green" woods, which are either still living or recently cut, are too wet to burn. In addition, hardwoods will burn more efficiently and are far better for flavor—softwoods (e.g. pine, spruce, and fir) will be very smoky when burned and impart a rancid flavor to food.

Baking Tips

The best vessel for baking with fire is a Dutch oven with lid. However, you also can wrap foods like fish or vegetables in foil, or rig up an improvised oven using a metal barrel or the metal basins in washing machines.

The best heat source for baking is coals or embers, which can go below and on top of your baking vessel to imitate oven conditions and provide a more even application of heat. Coals and embers will only last 15 to 30 minutes, so be sure to replenish as needed.

Judging Fire Temperature

The Hand Method

Estimate the temperature by holding an open palm three inches above the flames or coals. The length of time it takes for you to pull your hand away can tell the temperature:

- 500°F or hotter: 1 second or shorter
- 450 to 500°F: 1 to 2 seconds
- 400 to 450°F: 2 to 3 seconds
- 350 to 400°F: 4 to 5 seconds
- 300 to 350°F: 5 to 7 seconds
- 250 to 350°F: Longer than 7 seconds

The Coal Method

Use charcoal or let your fire burn down to coals. Estimate the temperature by evaluating the appearance of the coals:

- 500°F or hotter: Thin layer of white ash with a bright red glow on the coals
- 450 to 500°F: Thick layer of white ash with a bright red glow on the coals
- 400 to 450°F: Thick layer of white ash with a soft red glow on the coals
- 350 to 400°F: Thick layer of white ash with a soft yellow/brown glow on the coals

Chapter 2
Fueling Up for Survival

They say that breakfast is the most important meal of the day, and that's especially true when every meal could be your last. Make the most of every new day with these hearty breakfast recipes.

Lori's (Not So) God-awful Pancakes

Lori always insisted on making pancakes for Rick and Carl every weekend, because she wanted them to be the type of family that ate pancakes together on Sunday mornings. Even though Rick remembered the pancakes as being "god-awful," he cherished what they stood for in spite of how they tasted. Fortunately, this significantly more delicious recipe will give you both good memories and a tasty meal.

If you don't have buttermilk, add a little apple cider vinegar to regular milk. If you don't have fresh milk at all, use powdered. And while real maple syrup may not be an option at the end of the world, you might be able to scavenge some of the more shelf-stable corn syrup–based varieties.

PREP TIME: 10 MINUTES
COOK TIME: 15 MINUTES
YIELDS: 4 SERVINGS (ABOUT 8 PANCAKES)

2 cups flour
3 tablespoons sugar
1½ teaspoons baking powder
1½ teaspoons baking soda
1¼ teaspoons kosher salt
2 large eggs
2½ cups buttermilk
3 tablespoons melted butter
Vegetable oil, for drizzling

1. Preheat your pan over medium-low heat.
2. In a medium bowl, whisk together the flour, sugar, baking powder, baking soda, and salt. Set aside.
3. In a medium bowl, whisk the eggs until frothy. Whisk in the buttermilk until well incorporated, then whisk in the melted butter.
4. Add the wet ingredients to the dry, mixing until just incorporated and no dry flour patches remain. Don't over mix!
5. Drizzle some vegetable oil into the hot pan, using a piece of paper towel to lightly coat the bottom of the pan evenly.
6. Using a ladle, pour about ⅓ cup of batter into the middle of the pan, pouring all batter into the same spot and allowing it to spread naturally.
7. Do not flip your pancake until you see bubbles rising to the surface of the batter and bursting, and the bottoms are brown (you can sneak a peek by gently lifting up an edge with your spatula). Flip, then cook until the other side is lightly browned.

TIP: If you have access to an oven, you can keep the cooked pancakes warm on a sheet tray until the entire batch is ready.

West Georgia Correctional Facility Oatmeal

Beyond the obvious protection benefits, prisons are a great place to scavenge for shelf-stable foods. It's no surprise that the survivors ended up in one and found themselves frequently consuming a classic prison staple—oatmeal.

When stored correctly, oats remain safe to eat and maintain their nutritional value for upward of thirty years. Steel-cut oats, called for here, are often overlooked in the modern kitchen because they take more time to prepare than rolled or quick-cooking oats, but they have a delightfully nutty flavor and chewy texture. In a postapocalyptic world, powdered butter and milk can be used in place of fresh. You can also make a large batch of plain oatmeal at once and reheat smaller batches as needed.

PREP TIME: 10 MINUTES   COOK TIME: 15 TO 25 MINUTES   YIELDS: 4 SERVINGS

5¾ cups water
1½ cups steel-cut oats
¼ teaspoon kosher salt
1 tablespoon powdered butter, or fresh if available
1 tablespoon powdered milk, or fresh if available
4 teaspoons brown sugar
¼ cup raisins
Ground cinnamon for sprinkling

1. In a large saucepan, bring the water, oats, and salt to a boil. Reduce heat to low.
2. Keep your oats at a very gentle simmer, adjusting the heat as needed. Stir the oats occasionally, making sure to scrape the sides and bottom of the pot where stuff is likely to stick and burn. Simmer for about 15 minutes before checking doneness. The oats are ready when they are tender, thick, and creamy—this may take another 5 to 10 minutes.
3. Stir in the butter and milk. Divide the oatmeal between four bowls and sprinkle each with one teaspoon of brown sugar, one tablespoon of raisins, and cinnamon to taste.

The Kingdom's Breakfast Cobbler

In the Kingdom, they have cobbler at every meal, and now you can, too—that is, if King Ezekiel's trusted advisor Jerry is willing to share. Using eggs as a base and biscuits on top, you can add anything you like, limited only by what's growing in your garden and what protein you have available. This recipe makes use of simple veggies that the Kingdom would likely have on hand.

PREP TIME: 20 MINUTES
COOK TIME: 45 TO 60 MINUTES, MOSTLY INACTIVE
YIELDS: 4 TO 6 SERVINGS

Cobbler Base:
Two ½-inch slices slab bacon
6 eggs
¼ cup heavy cream
½ teaspoon salt
¼ teaspoon pepper
1 potato, cooked, peeled, and cubed
½ shallot, sliced
½ zucchini, sliced
½ red bell pepper, diced
2 sprigs fresh thyme

Biscuits:
1 cup all-purpose flour
1 teaspoon baking powder
1 teaspoon sugar
½ teaspoon kosher salt
¼ cup butter, melted and cooled
½ cup buttermilk (reconstituted powdered
    buttermilk, if necessary)

1. If the bacon has a rind, remove it. Working lengthwise down the slice, cut off thick matchsticks.
2. In a pan set over low heat, cook the bacon matchsticks slowly until most of the fat has rendered and they are crispy on all sides—about 5 to 7 minutes per side. Remove to a paper towel–lined plate or tray and let cool.
3. When cool, chop the bacon up into cubes and set aside.
4. Preheat the oven to 350°F.
5. Beat the eggs until light and frothy. Add the cream, salt, and pepper, and whisk to combine.
6. Mix in the vegetables and bacon, then transfer the mixture to a baking dish.
7. Whisk together the flour, baking powder, sugar, and salt. Fold in the melted butter and buttermilk until just combined.
8. Pinch pieces of the dough onto the egg mixture. Don't worry if there are bald spots.
9. Bake until the biscuit is golden brown and cooked through, 45 to 60 minutes. Let cool and set for 20 minutes before serving.

Homestead Home Fries

If there's one thing a traditional farming family like the Greenes knows, it's how to rise and shine in style. These hearty home fries round out any morning meal with enough energy for a day full of field tending, fence fixing, and walker trapping.

A perfect companion to farm-fresh eggs from the coop and some thick-cut toast, these seemingly simple fries are elevated by bell peppers, onions, and herbs from the garden. The fresh chives and the minced garlic that are added after the potatoes are roasted give them some extra kick, but if you prefer a mellower flavor, you can add the garlic before roasting.

PREP TIME: 15 MINUTES　　　　COOK TIME: 30 TO 40 MINUTES　　　　YIELDS: 4 SERVINGS

3 pounds fingerling potatoes, washed and cut into 1-inch pieces
1 sweet onion, large-diced
1 bell pepper, large-diced
4 tablespoons olive oil
Salt and black pepper
3 cloves garlic, finely minced
¼ cup fresh chives, minced

1. Preheat the oven to 350°F.
2. In a large mixing bowl, toss together the potatoes, sweet onion, and bell peppers with the olive oil and salt and pepper to taste.
3. Transfer to a large shallow roasting pan. Roast for about 30 minutes before checking doneness. Cook for another 10 to 15 minutes if needed.
4. When cooked through, remove from oven and add the garlic and chives. Toss to combine.
5. Taste and adjust the seasoning as needed. Drizzle with additional olive oil if the mixture looks dry.
6. Let cool for 5 minutes before serving. Enjoy alongside the Governor's Welcome Scramble and toasted Sanctuary Seeded Bread.

The Governor's Welcome Scramble

Even though Woodbury and its leader, the Governor, were hiding their insidious nature beneath an idyllic surface, that doesn't mean that every egg in town was a bad one. Take, for instance, the breakfast that the Governor prepared for Andrea and Michonne when they first arrived in Woodbury. The meal was a welcome one, even if the motivation was sinister.

You can add some extra punch to this basic scramble with any number of tasty additions—fresh herbs, sautéed veggies, cooked sausage crumbles—at the end of cooking, but sometimes keeping things pure and simple is the best way to go.

PREP TIME: 5 MINUTES   COOK TIME: 5 MINUTES   YIELDS: 4 SERVINGS

8 large eggs
Salt and black pepper
8 slices of bread
2 tablespoons butter, canned or fresh, depending on what is on hand

1. Preheat a nonstick frying pan over low heat.
2. In a medium bowl, whisk the eggs vigorously and thoroughly until light and foamy. Proper whisking should take at least a minute or two. Add salt and pepper to taste and whisk to combine.
3. Make your toast, and distribute the toast among the plates.
4. Add one tablespoon of the butter to the pan and swirl to cover the surface. The pan should be cool enough that the butter melts fairly quickly but does not burn while you do this.
5. Pour the whisked eggs into the center of the pan and let the mixture sit for a second.
6. Using a spatula, begin to stir the eggs gently, leaving nice big curds initially—you can break them up later if you'd like. Alternate between stirring and giving the eggs room to cook.
7. Just before the eggs are fully cooked, while there is still some runny egg in the pan, turn off the heat and add the remaining tablespoon of butter. Gently fold it in.
8. Taste and adjust the seasoning if necessary. Divide between four plates.

The Art of Peaceful Breakfast Patties

Eastman, seen in the Season 6 episode "Here's Not Here," lived off the grid long before walkers ruled the world. So it's no surprise he would have a handy supply of homemade breakfast patties featuring dried herbs, garlic, and onions from his garden. Since Eastman was a strict vegetarian who did not believe in killing, the patties he offered to Morgan during his stay were of the nonmeat variety.

This recipe also incorporates a very popular and shelf-stable meat alternative called TVP (textured vegetable protein) to give the patties a satisfying chew. It's a dried protein that needs to be reconstituted in hot water for a few minutes before using.

PREP TIME: 20 MINUTES   COOK TIME: 10 MINUTES   YIELDS: 4 SERVINGS

¾ cup dried TVP, reconstituted per package
   directions to make 1½ cups
¼ cup freeze-dried red kidney beans, rehydrated
   and mashed to make ½ cup
½ cup old-fashioned (rolled) oats
2 garlic cloves, pureed
½ shallot, shredded
1 carrot, shredded
2 teaspoons fresh sage, finely chopped
1 teaspoon fresh thyme, finely chopped
1 teaspoon dried fennel, finely chopped
Pinch of dried chile flakes
Pinch of ground allspice
2 tablespoons maple syrup, if available
1 tablespoon tamari
1 teaspoon salt
½ teaspoon fresh ground black pepper
1 tablespoon vegetable oil
2 tablespoons arrowroot powder

1. Add ¾ cup of the reconstituted TVP, along with all the other ingredients, to the bowl of a food processor and pulse until well combined and thick.
2. Transfer the mixture to a large mixing bowl and add the remaining TVP. Mix well to combine.
3. Divide the mixture into quarters. Form each quarter into a patty and gently lay on a plate. Refrigerate for one hour or freeze for later use.
4. Preheat a large skillet over medium-high heat. Once hot, add the vegetable oil.
5. Add two or three of the patties, without overcrowding. Fry the patties undisturbed until nicely browned, 2 to 4 minutes each side. Transfer cooked patties to a plate lined with paper towels.
6. Arrange the patties on a tray with tomato slices, a glass of powdered orange drink, and Homemade Chocolate Clusters.

Morgan's Peanut Butter Protein Bars

No matter what the mat by the door may say, no one is ever so welcome that they can help themselves to someone else's protein bars—especially the very last peanut butter one. Here's how to make your own no-bake version of this delicious treat.

PREP TIME: 10 MINUTES   COOK TIME: 10 MINUTES   INACTIVE TIME: 2 HOURS
YIELDS: 12 BARS

½ cup honey
¼ cup maple syrup
½ cup peanut butter (crunchy or smooth)
1 teaspoon cinnamon for dusting
3 cups puffed rice cereal
¼ cup protein powder
½ cup chocolate chips
¼ cup dried cranberries
¼ cup salted sunflower seeds

1. Line the bottom of a large glass baking dish with parchment paper, cutting it if necessary so that it fits the length of the pan and there is some overhang over the sides of the dish.
2. In a large saucepan, melt the honey, maple syrup, and peanut butter over medium heat, stirring occasionally until smooth and runny.
3. Remove from heat and stir in the cinnamon. Let cool for 10 minutes before proceeding, stirring occasionally.
4. Mix in the puffed rice cereal, protein powder, chocolate chips, dried cranberries, and sunflower seeds until everything is well combined and coated.
5. Spread the mixture onto the paper-lined baking dish, using a spatula to press it down firmly and create an even layer.
6. Allow the mixture to set in the fridge for 1 to 2 hours.
7. Remove from the fridge and use the parchment overhang to lift the mixture out of the dish and onto a cutting board. Remove the parchment paper and cut into 12 bars, making sure to properly hide one for later.

Foundational Fried SPAM®

SPAM® *is a surprisingly versatile shelf-stable meat worthy of stockpiling during any apocalypse. In fact, if the Governor was to be believed, the colony of Woodbury began thanks to a small handful of survivors "holed up in an apartment with* SPAM® *and Saltine crackers." This recipe offers a savory-sweet variation thanks to easy-to-find soy sauce packets and a little cayenne that will get your motor revving like Dale's RV on the best of days. But the meat at the recipe's foundation can be easily adapted to fit a wide variety of flavor profiles. Use maple and dried sage in place of the honey and cayenne and put it onto Dwight's Egg Sandwich, or cube it and serve alongside Homestead Home Fries or the Governor's Welcome Scramble.*

PREP TIME: 5 MINUTES   COOK TIME: 5 MINUTES   YIELDS: 4 TO 6 SERVINGS

One 1-tablespoon packet of soy sauce
2 tablespoons maple syrup
½ teaspoon garlic powder
⅛ teaspoon cayenne pepper
1 tablespoon oil
1 can SPAM® Classic

1. In a small bowl whisk together the soy sauce, maple syrup, garlic powder, and cayenne pepper.
2. Preheat a large pan over medium heat with the cooking oil.
3. Slice the SPAM® into 6 equal pieces.
4. Brush the glaze onto one side of the SPAM® slices. Then add them to the hot pan, glaze side down. Don't overcrowd the pan.
5. Fry in batches as small as two, if necessary. Fry until golden brown and crunchy, about 2 minutes. In the meantime, brush glaze onto the side facing up.
6. When browned, flip the SPAM® and reglaze the browned side. Once the other side is browned, flip once more and brush again with glaze. Serve hot.

Dwight's Egg Sandwich

Dwight learned firsthand just how cruel and ruthless this new world could be when Negan stole his wife, brutally disfigured him, and then forced him to become his loyal henchman. No one can blame Dwight for eating his feelings, but we can question his taste in sandwiches.

As it turns out, even though Dwight's egg sandwich may not be conventional, it does have a unique balance of sweet, sour, and savory that could make even the most downtrodden survivor forget their endless suffering.

PREP TIME: 5 MINUTES   COOK TIME: 5 MINUTES   YIELDS: 1 LONELY SANDWICH

Sanctuary Seeded Bread, sliced
1 tablespoon cooking oil
2 eggs
Salt and pepper
2 teaspoons yellow mustard
4 pieces bread-and-butter pickles
1 small tomato, sliced
1 large leaf of iceberg lettuce

1. Toast two slices of bread. Set aside.
2. Add the oil to a nonstick skillet and heat to low.
3. Crack the eggs into the pan. Cook until the whites are cooked through, about 2 minutes. Flip and cook another 2 minutes to medium-hard (or to your preference). Sprinkle with salt and pepper to taste.
4. Spread the mustard over each slice of bread.
5. Lay the pickles over one slice. Then, using a spatula, gently slip the eggs on top of the pickles.
6. Lay the tomatoes over the eggs. Season with salt and pepper to taste.
7. Cover with the leaf of lettuce, then top with the second piece of bread.

Chapter 3
Dig In! Meals for Hungry Survivors

There's no way of knowing what tomorrow will bring, so dig in!
Whether in the comfort of your own kitchen or around the campfire
at the end of civilization, gather friends and family and celebrate
making it to another meal with these recipes.

Amy and Andrea's Campfire Fish Fry

As previously noted, fishing is an extremely useful skill to have when society collapses. Amy and Andrea were once the heroes of their camp when they came home with a line full of crappie, bluegill, and freshwater drum in the Season 1 episode "Vatos." Even amid the chaos of the end of the world, these two sisters were still able to recall all that their father had taught them about angling.

If you can get out for some freshwater fishing—or you still have access to a quality seafood source—use this simple preparation for your catch of the day.

PREP TIME: 5 MINUTES   COOK TIME: 10 MINUTES   YIELDS: 4 SERVINGS

2 pounds fresh white fish, cleaned, scaled, and filleted (see "Fishing Basics" guide)
Salt and pepper
½ cup plus ½ teaspoon flour, divided
4 tablespoons vegetable oil
¼ cup fish stock
1 tablespoon lemon juice
1 tablespoon butter
1 tablespoon fresh parsley, chopped

1. Pat both sides of the fish dry, then season the nonskin side with salt and pepper to taste.
2. Dredge each fillet in ½ cup of flour, shaking off the excess.
3. Heat a large skillet with two tablespoons of oil over medium heat. A nonstick pan will help keep the fish from sticking, but a cast iron or stainless steel skillet will give you a better crispiness. The pan is ready when a flick of water sizzles on contact.
4. Add as many filets as will comfortably fit in the pan; do not crowd them. Put the fish into the pan, skin side down, and leave undisturbed for 2 to 3 minutes until nicely browned and cooked partially through.
5. Using a spatula, gently flip the fish over and let cook for another 2 to 3 minutes; cook time will vary depending on the thickness of your fillet. The fish is ready when it is opaque throughout and flakes easily. Gently remove from the pan and set aside.
6. Add ½ teaspoon of flour to the pan and mix constantly for 15 to 30 seconds until browned.
7. Add the fish stock to the hot pan to deglaze, scraping up all the tasty brown bits at the bottom of the pan. Let the stock reduce and thicken, 1 to 2 minutes.
8. Turn off the heat then add the lemon juice and butter and stir to combine. Taste and adjust seasoning as needed.
9. Sprinkle the plated fish with the parsley and spoon the pan sauce onto each.

Dixon Deer Stew

We all know that Daryl Dixon is a natural tracker and hunter. He'd also be the first to tell you that a deer is far more than just tenderloin and chops. To make the most of the whole animal, you are going to have to use up those tougher cuts from the shoulder and rear. These cuts are perfect for stewing because of all the connective tissue that breaks down over long cooking and causes the meat to become fork-tender.

If you can't get your hands on venison, you can substitute stewing beef—at least until you get your hunting skills up to snuff (see "Hunting Basics") or make it to your local butcher. This recipe features simple vegetables the group could have grown in their prison garden: onions, carrots, potatoes, and peas. In nonapocalyptic settings, feel free to add more "exotic" ingredients like button mushrooms or parsnips.

PREP TIME: 10 MINUTES   **COOK TIME: 2 HOURS**   **YIELDS: 4 SERVINGS**

3 tablespoons olive or vegetable oil

3 pounds venison stew meat (from the front shoulder or rear end: chuck roast, top round, bottom round), cubed

Salt and pepper

2 sweet onions, diced

2 cloves garlic, minced

3 tablespoons flour

1 tablespoon tomato paste

1¼ cups red wine for deglazing, or water

4½ cups beef broth, divided

1 teaspoon dried thyme

1 bay leaf, if available

3 carrots, peeled and sliced into ½-inch rounds

2 large potatoes, diced

½ cup barley

½ cup peas, garden fresh or frozen

1. Preheat a large heavy pot (like a Dutch oven, if available) with 1 tablespoon of oil over medium-high heat.
2. Pat the meat dry and season generously with salt and pepper, to taste.
3. Cover the bottom of the pot with a single layer of meat—do not overcrowd it or it will not sear properly. Leave the meat undisturbed for 3 to 5 minutes, until it has nicely browned.
4. Repeat for all sides, remove from the pot, and set aside.
5. Repeat the process for the remaining meat, adding another tablespoon of oil if needed. You will see a brown mess at the bottom of the pan—this is a good sign. If it begins to burn, turn down the heat.
6. Turn the heat down to medium. Add another tablespoon of oil, if needed, along with the onions, and stir until softened, about 5 minutes.
7. Add the garlic and stir until fragrant.
8. Add the flour and cook, stirring constantly, for 2 minutes.
9. Add the tomato paste and stir constantly for another minute.
10. Turn the heat to high and add the red wine, working up all the browned bits at the bottom of the pot with your spoon.
11. Return the meat to the pot, and cover with 4 cups of broth. Add the thyme and bay leaf.
12. Bring to a boil, then turn the heat down, cover, and simmer for 1 hour.
13. Stir in the carrots and potatoes. Simmer covered for another 30 minutes.
14. Add the barley to the pot, along with ½ cup of broth. Simmer covered for another 30 minutes.
15. Check the doneness of both the meat and the barley. The stew is done when everything is tender. Stir in the peas, cover, and let sit for 5 minutes.
16. Taste and adjust the seasoning if necessary.

Oceanside Fish Stew

When Tara washed up on the shore of the secretive Oceanside community, she was probably too disoriented to realize that she had struck seafood gold. The salted perch Oceanside resident Cyndie left for her was an indicator that being so close to the Atlantic meant the women of Oceanside had access to ample saltwater fish. Tara soon found herself enjoying a hearty fish stew for dinner with Oceanside leader Natania and her group.

This Oceanside homage is chock-full of shellfish and other kinds of seafood. You can adjust your marine protein based on availability and personal preferences. If using clams, soak them in cool water for 20 to 30 minutes and give their shells a good scrub. For mussels, clean off their shells and remove the bristly beards that line their exteriors.

Even if you've been sworn to secrecy, this is one dish you won't be able to resist telling everyone about!

PREP TIME: 15 MINUTES   COOK TIME: 1 HOUR   YIELDS: 4 SERVINGS

4 whole anchovies

4 cloves garlic, pureed

1 teaspoon salt, plus more for seasoning the fish

2 sprigs fresh oregano

2 sprigs fresh thyme

1 sprig fresh parsley

1 bay leaf

2 tablespoons olive oil

½ sweet onion, diced

2 ribs celery, sliced

2 carrots, sliced

1 tablespoon tomato paste

½ teaspoon crushed chile flakes

1 cup dry white wine

One 28-ounce can crushed tomatoes

4 cups water

½ pound fingerling potatoes, cut into ½-inch pieces

1 pound clams, soaked in saltwater and cleaned

1 pound mussels, cleaned and debearded

½ pound medium tail-on shrimp, peeled and deveined

½ pound flaky white fish such as bass, halibut, or cod, cut into 1-inch pieces

Ground pepper

1. In a small bowl, mash the anchovies with the pureed garlic and 1 teaspoon of salt until well incorporated. Set aside.
2. Tie the sprigs of oregano, thyme, and parsley, and the bay leaf together with butcher twine. Set aside.
3. In a large saucepan, heat the olive oil over a medium-high heat. Add the onion, celery, and carrots. Stir frequently until the onion has softened, about 5 minutes.
4. Add the anchovy mixture and stir until fragrant, about 15 seconds.
5. Add the tomato paste and chile flakes and cook, stirring frequently, for another minute.
6. Turn the heat to high and add the wine, tomatoes, water, tied herbs, and potatoes. Bring to a boil and then reduce to medium-low heat to simmer for 30 minutes.
7. Remove the herbs and discard. Taste and adjust the seasoning as needed.
8. Stir in the cleaned clams and let simmer for 2 minutes. Stir in the mussels and shrimp.
9. Season the white fish with salt and pepper to taste, then arrange the pieces on top of the stew.
10. Cover the pot and let simmer until the shellfish have opened and the fish is opaque and flaky, another 5 to 7 minutes.
11. Serve with freshly baked Sanctuary Seeded Bread to soak up all the delicious broth.

Carol's Spring Cleaning Casserole

In her effort to use the canned foods that no one in Alexandria seemed to want, Carol planned to whip up a "spring cleaning casserole" in the Season 6 episode "JSS." Though the Alexandrians sadly never got to find out just how tasty her creation was, now is your chance to try the same thing.

To create this dish, go ahead and use up whatever forgotten cans of vegetables and beans you might have lurking at the back of the shelf, and feel free to play with the seasonings and even the type of creamed soup as desired.

PREP TIME: 10 MINUTES   COOK TIME: 40 MINUTES   YIELDS: 6 TO 8 SERVINGS

1 medium sweet onion, diced
2 tablespoons olive oil
One 15-ounce can water chestnuts, drained
Two 15-ounce cans mixed vegetables, drained
One 15-ounce can cream of celery soup
1 cup mayonnaise
¾ teaspoon smoked paprika
Black pepper
1½ cups crackers, crushed

1. Preheat the oven to 350°F.
2. In a medium sauté pan over medium-high heat, cook the onions in the olive oil until they soften and start to brown, about 5 minutes.
3. In a large mixing bowl, toss together the sautéed onion, water chestnuts, mixed vegetables, cream of celery soup, mayonnaise, and smoked paprika. Season with black pepper to taste.
4. Transfer to a large baking dish and sprinkle with the crushed crackers.
5. Bake until hot, bubbling, and browned on top, about 35 to 40 minutes. Let the casserole cool for 15 minutes before serving.

Zucchini Noodles with Tomato and Pine Nuts

Zucchini is easy to grow, and a small crop produces enough vegetables to satisfy a hungry community and the demands of their so-called Saviors. There are so many ways to use zucchini—in baked goods, in soups, or in a Roasted Garden Vegetable Medley. But if you can get your hands on a kitchen gadget known as a spiralizer, you can quickly and easily make enough zucchini noodles—also known as "zoodles"—to feed your entire group.

This is a no-cook recipe, perfect for when you want a light meal or need to preserve generator power. You can even use it to make noodles from any number of veggies, including beets and carrots.

PREP TIME: 30 MINUTES   COOK TIME: N/A   YIELDS: 4 SERVINGS

1 pint cherry tomatoes
1 teaspoon salt
3 Roma tomatoes, roughly chopped
2 garlic cloves, crushed
½ cup toasted pine nuts, divided
½ teaspoon chile flakes
1 cup basil leaves, hand torn, divided
4 ounces canned pumpkin puree
2 pounds spiraled zucchini (about 4 medium zucchini)
¼ cup olive oil

1. Half the cherry tomatoes and add them to a large mixing bowl. Salt lightly and set aside.
2. Add the Roma tomatoes, garlic, half of the pine nuts (¼ cup), chile flakes, half the basil (½ cup), salt, and pumpkin puree to the bowl of a food processor or blender. Pulse until smooth.
3. Add the mixture to the bowl of cherry tomatoes.
4. Add the zucchini and olive oil to the bowl. Toss well to combine. Taste and, if necessary, adjust the seasoning.
5. Divide among four plates. Sprinkle with the remaining pine nuts and hand-torn basil.

Aaron and Eric's Linguine

No one would blame Daryl for hastily slurping down an entire plate of Aaron and Eric's saucy linguine or wiping his mouth on his sleeve. After a day of hunting to help support his new home at Alexandria, he would have been famished! One taste of this recipe, and you're bound to do the same (but perhaps you might consider using a napkin instead of your sleeve).

This sauce makes use of sun-dried tomatoes (see our "Food Preservation" guide). In the absence of appropriate weather or drying racks, you can easily make the sun-dried tomatoes for this recipe in the oven. With the oven set to 200°F, they should take about 6 to 8 hours and will taste nearly as good as if they'd been dried outside in the pure sunshine.

PREP TIME: 10 MINUTES   COOK TIME: 30 MINUTES   YIELDS: 4 SERVINGS

3 tablespoons olive oil, divided
1 small sweet onion, minced
2 cloves garlic, minced
One 28-ounce can crushed tomatoes
1 cup sun-dried cherry tomatoes
1 bay leaf
Salt and pepper
1 cup breadcrumbs, preferably panko
1 pound uncooked linguine

1. Set a large pot of water for the pasta to boil.
2. Heat a medium saucepan over medium heat and add 2 tablespoons of the olive oil. Sweat the minced onion, stirring frequently, until soft and translucent, about 2 minutes.
3. Add the minced garlic and stir until fragrant, about 10 seconds.
4. Turn the heat to high, and add both kinds of tomato and the bay leaf. Season with salt and pepper to taste.
5. Bring to a boil, then reduce heat to low and simmer.
6. In a medium skillet, mix together the breadcrumbs and the remaining tablespoon of olive oil over medium heat. Season with salt and pepper to taste.
7. Stir constantly until the breadcrumbs are golden brown and evenly toasted. Remove from the pan and set aside.
8. Cook the linguine according to package directions. Drain and return to the pot.
9. Remove the bay leaf from the sauce, taste, and, if necessary, adjust the seasoning.
10. Add a few ladlefuls of sauce to the pot of pasta, and use tongs to toss and coat evenly.
11. Divide the pasta among four plates and top each with an additional ladle of sauce. Sprinkle each serving with ¼ cup of toasted breadcrumbs.

Hershel's Spaghetti Tuesday Dinner

In honor of the late, beloved Hershel Greene, we hereby declare that every Wednesday should be Spaghetti Tuesday. All you need to do is find some spaghetti. Add some farm-fresh tomatoes—cooked quickly to preserve their sun-ripened flavor and accented by sweet onion and fresh basil—for a simply delicious sauce that would have made Hershel proud.

PREP TIME: 30 MINUTES   COOK TIME: 10 MINUTES   YIELDS: 4 SERVINGS

5 pounds fresh Roma tomatoes
3 tablespoons unsalted butter
1 medium sweet onion, diced
Salt and pepper to taste
1 pound dried spaghetti
2 sprigs fresh basil

1. Bring a large pot of water to a rolling boil. Set up an ice bath in a large bowl.
2. Score an "X" on the bottom of each tomato.
3. Add the tomatoes to the boiling water and blanch for 30 seconds. (If needed, work in batches so as not to overcrowd the pot.) Using tongs, remove each tomato from the hot water and drop it into the ice bath. As soon as the tomato is cool enough to handle, remove it from the ice bath.
4. Working from the scored "X," peel each tomato using a paring knife.
5. Cut each tomato in half lengthwise and, using a spoon, scoop out the seeds. Rough chop the tomatoes into ½-inch pieces. Set aside.
6. In a large saucepan, melt the butter over low heat. Add the onion and sweat it until the pieces are soft and translucent, about 5 minutes.
7. Add the tomatoes and turn the heat up to medium-high. Season with salt and pepper to taste.
8. Bring the sauce to a boil, then reduce the heat, cover, and simmer for 15 minutes.
9. Bring a large pot of water to a boil. When the sauce has about 10 or so minutes left to simmer, add a small palmful of salt to the pot of water and return to a boil before adding the pasta.
10. Cook the spaghetti until it is al dente, according to the package directions. Strain and return to the pot.
11. Taste the sauce and, if necessary, adjust the seasoning. Hand-tear the basil into the sauce, and stir to combine.
12. Add a couple of ladles of sauce to the pasta, mix to combine.
13. Divide the pasta among four plates. Pour a ladleful of sauce atop each.

Homemade S'Getti Rings

Tara and her family survived on a stockpile of canned Gorbelli S'Getti Rings for some time, but they weren't nearly as excited about them as Abraham was when he found a can in an abandoned RV in the Season 5 episode "The Distance."

This homemade version is a dead ringer for the canned variety, without the high sodium and preservatives.

PREP TIME: 10 MINUTES   COOK TIME: 40 MINUTES   YIELDS: 4 SERVINGS

½ medium sweet onion, minced
2 tablespoons canned butter (fresh if available)
2 tablespoons tomato paste
½ teaspoon onion powder
½ teaspoon garlic powder
¼ teaspoon paprika
One 28-ounce can tomato puree
1½ teaspoons salt, plus more for cooking the pasta
½ teaspoon fresh ground pepper
2 tablespoons sugar
½ pound uncooked anelletti (small, thin rings of pasta)

1. Heat a medium saucepan over low heat. Melt the butter and add the onion. Cook, stirring occasionally, until very soft and translucent, about 5 minutes.
2. Add the tomato paste, onion powder, garlic powder, and paprika. Stir to combine and cook for another minute.
3. Add the tomato puree, salt, pepper, and sugar. Stir to combine.
4. Adjust heat to medium high, bring to a boil, then reduce heat to medium low and let simmer while you cook the pasta.
5. Bring a large pot of water to a rolling boil. Add small palmful of salt to the water and return to boil before adding the pasta.
6. Cook pasta until al dente, according to package directions. Drain the pasta well.
7. Taste the sauce and adjust seasoning if needed.
8. Mix in the cooked pasta and stir to combine. Divide among four bowls.

Negan's Spaghetti all'Arrabbiata

The Italian word arrabbiata translates to "angry," so it was a fitting sauce to prepare when Negan commandeered Rick's kitchen to host an impromptu dinner in the Season 7 episode "Hearts Still Beating." This classic sauce is known for its spicy kick, so if there's no discomfort level when you eat it, then you probably need to add more chile.

For a full on The Walking Dead *dining experience, serve this dish with Carl's Biscuits and Alexandria Lemonade.*

PREP TIME: 10 MINUTES   COOK TIME: 30 MINUTES   YIELDS: 4 SERVINGS

2 tablespoons olive oil
3 cloves garlic, finely sliced
1½ tablespoons tomato paste
1 teaspoon dried chile flakes, or more to taste
One 26-ounce can chopped tomatoes
Salt
1 pound dried spaghetti

1. Heat a large saucepan over low heat. Add the olive oil and swirl to coat the pan.
2. Add the garlic and stir frequently until softened, about 3 minutes.
3. Turn the heat up to medium-high, then add the tomato paste and chile flakes, stirring constantly until fragrant and dark red, 1 to 2 minutes.
4. Add the canned tomato and stir until well combined. Season with salt to taste.
5. Bring the sauce to a boil, then reduce the heat and simmer for 20 minutes. Remove from heat.
6. Bring a large pot of water to a rolling boil. Add a small palmful of salt to the pot and return to a boil before adding the pasta.
7. Cook the spaghetti until al dente, according to the package directions. Strain and return to the pot.
8. Add a couple of ladlefuls of sauce to the pasta, and mix to combine.
9. Divide the pasta among four plates. Pour a ladleful of sauce atop each.

Greene Family Farm Roast Chicken

The Greene family farm seemed like a little slice of pastoral heaven when Rick's group first arrived there in Season 2—at least until someone opened up the barn. . . . While there, the survivors enjoyed fresh fruits and vegetables from the land, milk from cows, eggs from chickens, and even meat that wasn't squirrel! In the right setting, something as simple as a well-roasted chicken can become a thing of true beauty.

The first trick to this recipe is using a spatchcocked chicken, in which the backbone has been removed from a whole chicken so that it can be laid flat. This is useful because it means a more even surface and more even cooking, since different parts of a whole bird cook at different speeds. Ask your butcher, who will be happy to spatchcock your bird for you.

The second trick is to weigh down the chicken so that all the skin get super crispy. Often this method of roasting chicken is called "brick chicken" or "chicken under a brick," because traditionally it involves weighing the bird down with foil-wrapped bricks—but you can use another heavy skillet filled with canned food if you can't get your hands on bricks.

PREP TIME: 5 MINUTES   COOK TIME: 30 MINUTES   YIELDS: 4 SERVINGS

1 whole chicken, spatchcocked
4 tablespoons olive oil
1 teaspoon fresh rosemary, chopped very finely
1 teaspoon fresh marjoram, chopped
1 teaspoon fresh thyme, chopped
2 teaspoons salt
¼ teaspoon pepper
2 garlic cloves, crushed
Sprigs of fresh herbs for the pan

1. Rinse the chicken and pat dry with paper towels.
2. Mix together 1 tablespoon of the olive oil, the fresh herbs, salt, and pepper. Using your hands, rub this all over the chicken.
3. Preheat the oven to 375°F.
4. Heat an ovenproof skillet (such as cast iron) over medium-high heat with the remaining 3 tablespoons of oil. When the pan is nearly smoking, add the chicken skin side down.
5. Put a second large skillet on top of the chicken and add the foil-covered bricks. Make sure the weight is evenly distributed, or the skin will crisp up only in the center.
6. Turn the heat down to low and let the skin crisp for 20 minutes. You'll hear a lot of bubbling and boiling action—this is normal. After 20 minutes, check to see that the skin is golden brown and crackly throughout. If it's not, recover and cook for another 10 minutes.
7. Carefully loosen the crispy skin from the bottom of the pan before flipping the chicken over.
8. Add the crushed garlic cloves and sprigs of fresh herbs.
9. Transfer the chicken to the oven to finish cooking for another 10 to 15 minutes, or until the juices run clear and it is cooked through. Let rest for 5 minutes before carving and serving.

Chicken à la Lucille

Need to work out some aggression? Pounding the chicken in this recipe with a blunt instrument tenderizes the meat through sheer brute force. It also evens out the thickness of the meat and allows it to cook more uniformly, which ultimately means a juicier breast. For best results, a mallet or heavy pan is recommended instead of a barb wire-wrapped baseball bat. But if Lucille is hungry, well, it's unlikely that anyone is going to stop her.

PREP TIME: 10 MINUTES
COOK TIME: 10 MINUTES
YIELDS: 4 SERVINGS

4 boneless, skinless chicken breasts
1 cup all-purpose flour
Salt
Black pepper
3 eggs
1½ cups panko breadcrumbs
¼ cup Parmesan, grated
1 teaspoon fresh parsley, chopped
2 tablespoons olive oil
2 tablespoons butter

1. Put one breast between two pieces of parchment paper. Using a mallet, a baseball bat, or a heavy saucepan, pound the breast until it is uniformly thin, about ¼ inch thick. Repeat with the remaining breasts.
2. Add the flour to a shallow rimmed dish or container, sprinkle with salt and pepper to taste, and mix to combine.
3. Beat the eggs in a second shallow rimmed dish until light and frothy.
4. Add the breadcrumbs, Parmesan, and fresh parsley to a third shallow rimmed dish, and mix to combine.
5. Arrange the three pans in a row. Dip the chicken in the seasoned flour, then the eggs, and finally the breadcrumbs to coat evenly. Repeat for all the breasts.
6. Heat the butter and olive oil in a large skillet or frying pan over medium heat.
7. Gently lower 1 or 2 breasts into the pan, being sure not to overcrowd them. Cook until golden brown, about 3 minutes per side. Repeat with the remaining breasts.
8. Lay the cooked breasts onto a tray lined with paper towel to absorb excess oil.

Curried Goat Stew

Even though the strictly vegetarian Eastman may have been fundamentally against eating his beloved goat, Tabitha, there's no question that goats would make great livestock to raise following a walker apocalypse, for both their milk and their meat, and the cheese made from their milk.

Goat meat is a staple in many cuisines, including African, Middle Eastern, and Indian. This stew features classic Indian spices that accentuate the flavorful goat meat perfectly. When chopped up finely and simmered for hours, tough goat stew meat will melt in your mouth.

PREP TIME: 20 MINUTES   COOK TIME: 2 HOURS, 15 MINUTES   YIELDS: 4 SERVINGS

2 tablespoons olive oil
3 pounds goat stew meat, small-diced
Salt
1 teaspoon ground cumin
2 teaspoons curry powder
1 teaspoon garam masala
1 teaspoon paprika
1 tablespoon tomato paste
1 medium sweet onion, quartered and sliced
2 cloves garlic, minced
1 tablespoon grated fresh ginger
2 Yukon potatoes, cut into ½-inch cubes
One 28-ounce can crushed tomatoes
8 cups beef or chicken broth
1 bay leaf
1 stick cinnamon
2 tablespoons fresh cilantro, chopped

1. Add the olive oil to a large saucepan and heat over medium heat.
2. Liberally salt the goat meat to taste, then add about half of the meat to the hot pan, being sure not to overcrowd. Cook until nicely browned on all sides, about 6 minutes. Remove from pan and set aside. Repeat with the remaining meat.
3. In a small bowl, combine the cumin, curry powder, garam masala, and paprika.
4. Add the spice blend to the pan and stir constantly until toasted and fragrant, about a minute.
5. Add the tomato paste, onion, garlic, and ginger to the saucepan. Stir until fragrant.
6. Add the potatoes, tomatoes, broth, bay leaf, and cinnamon stick to the pan. Stir to combine.
7. Return the goat meat to the pan. Bring the stew to a boil, then cover and reduce to a simmer for about 90 minutes, or until the goat is fork-tender. Stir the stew occasionally and top up with more broth if needed.
8. When done, remove the bay leaf and cinnamon stick. Garnish with the fresh cilantro.
9. Serve with rice or Seeded Sanctuary Bread.

Rick's Cucumber and Onion Salad

During the group's time at the prison, Rick temporarily stepped down as leader and focused on farming instead. He hoped to give Carl a more "normal" slice of life, growing cucumbers and tending to their pigs. Sadly, Rick's pastoral reprieve was short-lived, and it was surely hard for him to abandon his impressive cucumber crop when the Governor ultimately sent the survivors scattering into the nearby woods.

This simple cucumber salad uses a very traditional Southern preparation, perfect to serve alongside Greene Family Farm Roast Chicken and some of Carl's Biscuits.

PREP TIME: 10 MINUTES   COOK TIME: 5 MINUTES   INACTIVE TIME: 1 HOUR
YIELDS: 4 SERVINGS

2 medium cucumbers, peeled and sliced ¼-inch thick
Kosher salt, to taste
½ cup apple cider vinegar
½ cup water
1 tablespoon granulated sugar
½ teaspoon celery seed
1 medium sweet onion, quartered and sliced ¼-inch thick
Freshly ground black pepper

1. Put the sliced cucumbers into a large mixing bowl. Sprinkle liberally with salt to taste, toss, and set aside.
2. Combine the vinegar, water, sugar, and celery seed in a small saucepan. Heat over medium until steaming, but do not boil.
3. Add the sliced onions to the cucumbers, then cover with the dressing. Let them sit for at least an hour before serving, or cover and let them sit overnight in the fridge.
4. Toss and season with pepper to taste before serving.

Tara's Turkey Chili

When we first met Tara, her family had been surviving not only on S'Getti Rings but also Gorbelli Turkey Chili and other canned delicacies that they were able to scavenge from her father's food delivery truck.

This homemade version of that chili is savory and filling, perfect for when you need an extra boost of energy to flee or fight. Using dried chiles gives this recipe a better depth of flavor, but you can substitute three tablespoons of chile powder if you must.

PREP TIME: 20 MINUTES   COOK TIME: 1 HOUR   YIELDS: 6 SERVINGS

1 dried ancho chile
3 dried chiles de árbol
5 dried chipotle chiles
1 teaspoon coriander seeds
1 teaspoon ground cumin
1 teaspoon dried thyme
1 teaspoon dried oregano
3 garlic cloves
Two 28-ounce cans crushed tomatoes
2 tablespoons olive oil

1 pound ground turkey
1 medium sweet onion, minced
2 stalks celery, sliced
1 red bell pepper, diced
2 jalapeños, sliced
2 cups chicken broth or stock
1 bay leaf
One 15-ounce can kidney beans, drained
One 15-ounce can pinto beans, drained
Salt and pepper

1. In a heatproof bowl, cover the dried chiles with hot water and set aside.
2. To the bowl of a food processor or blender, add the coriander, cumin, thyme, oregano, garlic, and ½ can of tomatoes.
3. When the dried chiles are soft and pliable, remove the stems and seeds.
4. Add the chiles to the food processor or blender. Pulse until smooth. Set aside.
5. In a large saucepot heat the olive oil on medium-high. Add the turkey meat and stir occasionally until nicely browned, about 8 minutes. Remove with a slotted spoon and set aside.
6. Add the onion to the saucepot and stir occasionally until it begins to soften, about 2 minutes.
7. Add the celery, bell pepper, and jalapeños, and cook until they begin to soften, another 2 minutes.
8. Add the meat back to the pot along with the pureed chile mixture and cook, stirring frequently, for 2 minutes.
9. Add the remaining crushed tomatoes, broth, and bay leaf. Add salt and pepper to taste.
10. Bring to a boil, then reduce the heat to medium-low. Add the beans, stir to combine, and simmer uncovered for an hour.
11. Taste and adjust the seasoning as needed. Serve with shredded cheese and sour cream, if they're available.

Bean Salad with Crispy Chickpeas

Dried beans are a great nonperishable food to have on hand. While they may be more labor intensive than their canned cousins, they're far more shelf-stable and tend to have a better texture and flavor. An excellent source of protein, fiber, and vitamins, dried beans are a must-add to your scavenging list. Plus, if you're stocking up before end times, dried beans are a much more economical choice than canned.

Making a bland, boring bean salad wouldn't win you any fans at Alexandria's next potluck dinner, however, so this festive recipe adds a bit of spice that will help you earn the praise of your fellow survivors.

PREP TIME: 30 MINUTES   COOK TIME: 50 MINUTES   YIELDS: 4 TO 6 SERVINGS

2 cups chickpeas, soaked overnight
  and cooked until tender
¼ teaspoon cayenne pepper
¼ teaspoon cumin
¼ cup plus 2 tablespoons olive oil
1½ teaspoons plus ¼ teaspoon salt
½ cup lemon juice
3 cloves garlic, pureed
½ teaspoon black pepper

1 cup black beans, soaked overnight
  and cooked until tender
2 cups kidney beans, soaked overnight
  and cooked until tender
½ medium red onion, finely minced
1 medium cucumber, peeled and finely diced
1 red bell pepper, finely diced
¾ cup parsley, finely chopped
¼ cup mint, finely chopped

1. Preheat the oven to 400°F.
2. Add the chickpeas to a medium mixing bowl. Toss with the cayenne pepper, cumin, 2 tablespoons of the olive oil, and ¼ teaspoon of the salt.
3. Spread the chickpeas out onto a parchment-lined baking sheet and roast, stirring every 10 minutes, until golden brown and crunchy all the way through, about 40 minutes. Remove from the oven and set aside to cool.
4. In a small bowl, whisk together the remaining ¼ cup olive oil, lemon juice, garlic, the remaining 1½ teaspoons salt, and pepper until well incorporated. Alternatively, use a blender or food processor.
5. Add the black and kidney beans, onion, cucumber, bell pepper, parsley, and mint to a large serving bowl.
6. Pour ¾ of the dressing over the beans, then toss well to combine.
7. Let the salad marinate for at least 20 minutes. Taste and adjust the seasoning if necessary. Add the remaining dressing, if needed.
8. Top the salad with the crunchy chickpeas just before serving.
9. Avoid refrigerating the salad if possible, or bring it to room temperature before serving if you do refrigerate.

DIY Grain Bowl

Life on the road has forced Rick and his comrades to become endlessly adaptable, and this healthy meal reflects that need. You can vary the recipe depending on what you have available and, as long as you stick to the simple formula of GRAIN + VEGETABLE + PROTEIN, *you will have a balanced meal, no matter how you assemble it.*

Grains can include rice, quinoa, bulgur, barley, farro, or wheat berries—all of which can be packed for long-term storage in a well-stocked survival cache (see "Survival Caches" guide). Vegetables can include whatever you have in season in your garden or what you have stored for the winter. Protein can include your latest catch, a poached egg, beans, or a textured vegetable protein. Be creative!

PREP TIME: 10 MINUTES   COOK TIME: 45 TO 55 MINUTES   YIELDS: 4 BOWLS

3 cups Jerusalem artichokes, peeled and diced
¾ cup vegetable oil, divided
1½ teaspoons salt, plus more for seasoning
   the eggs
½ teaspoon ground black pepper, plus more
   for seasoning the eggs
1 medium onion, diced
4 cups chard, washed and rough-chopped,
   including stems

½ cup apple cider vinegar, plus a dash
2 teaspoons mustard
2 tablespoons honey
1 teaspoon minced shallot
1 clove garlic, pureed
1 teaspoon hot sauce
4 cups cooked brown rice
1 tablespoon toasted, rough-chopped walnuts
4 eggs

1. Preheat the oven to 350°F. Line a baking sheet with parchment paper.
2. Toss the Jerusalem artichokes with 2 tablespoons of the oil, ½ teaspoon of salt, and ½ teaspoon of black pepper. Spread artichokes onto the parchment-lined baking sheet.
3. Roast the artichokes, stirring once, for 30 minutes or until tender and nicely browned.
4. In the meantime, heat 2 tablespoons of the remaining oil in a large skillet over medium heat. Add the onion and sweat until soft and translucent, about 5 minutes.
5. Turn the heat up to medium-high and add the chard. Cover and cook until slightly wilted but still bright green, about 2 minutes. Transfer to a bowl and set aside.
6. In a medium bowl combine the ½ cup of vinegar, mustard, honey, remaining salt, shallot, garlic, and hot sauce. Whisk until well combined. Gradually whisk in the remaining ½ cup of oil until the mixture is thick and fully combined. Alternatively, combine all the ingredients in a food processor or blender and pulse until smooth.
7. Put a small saucepan filled with water onto a medium-low heat.
8. Divide the cooked rice among four bowls. Drizzle each with 1 tablespoon of dressing. Add the cooked chard to one half of each bowl, and add the roasted Jerusalem artichokes to the other. Sprinkle with the chopped nuts.
9. Adjust the heat of the small saucepan so there is a very gentle simmer. Pour in a small dash of vinegar. Stir the water several times and add an egg. Cook for 2 minutes.
10. Using a slotted spoon, transfer it to one of the bowls. Season the egg lightly with salt and pepper to taste. Drizzle with another tablespoon of dressing.
11. Repeat with the remaining 3 eggs and bowls.

Wild Boar Chops with Juniper, Apples, and Sage

The citizens of the Kingdom have become adept at hunting a wide variety of local fauna—including wild boar. A wild pig tastes a lot like traditional pork, but the flavor is more complex and savory (and the ones that Ezekiel sent to Negan had a unique flavor all their own). Until the world ends, you should be able to hunt down boar rib chops from specialty butcher shops, or ask your butcher to special-order them for you. You can also substitute pork rib chops for boar if necessary.

PREP TIME: 4½ HOURS, MOSTLY INACTIVE   COOK TIME: 20 MINUTES   YIELDS: 4 SERVINGS

4 cups water, divided

4 tablespoons salt, plus more for seasoning the meat

½ teaspoon juniper berries, crushed

½ teaspoon black peppercorns

1 bay leaf

2 cloves garlic, crushed

4 wild boar rib chops

Ground black pepper

2 tablespoons olive oil

¾ cup chicken broth

½ cup apple cider

1 tablespoon Dijon mustard

1 Granny Smith apple, peeled, cored, and sliced

½ large sweet onion, sliced

2 tablespoons fresh sage, roughly chopped

1. In a medium saucepan, bring to a boil 1 cup of the water with 4 tablespoons of salt, the juniper berries, peppercorns, and bay leaf.
2. Remove from the heat and add the remaining 3 cups of cool water and the crushed garlic. The brine should be about room temperature.
3. Lay the chops out in a shallow roasting pan or baking dish and cover with the brine. The meat should be covered. If not, make additional liquid with a ratio of 1 cup water to 1 tablespoon salt.
4. Brine the chops for at least 30 minutes, ideally 4 hours.
5. Preheat the oven to 350°F.
6. Remove the chops from the brine and pat dry. Season with salt and pepper to taste.
7. Heat a large skillet with 1 tablespoon of the olive oil over medium-high heat. Add 1 or 2 chops, making sure not to crowd them. Sear each side until it is golden brown, about 2 minutes per side. Transfer the chops to a large baking dish or sheet tray lined with parchment. Repeat with the remaining chops.
8. Using a meat thermometer, check the internal temperature of the chops before putting them in the oven. Medium-rare chops should have an internal temperature of about 140°F. Finish the chops in the oven, cooking for another 2 to 3 minutes. The temperature will continue to rise to about 145°F while resting. Let the chops rest for about 5 minutes before serving.
9. While the chops are finishing in the oven and resting, use the pan you seared the chops in to make the sauce. Combine the broth, apple cider, and Dijon mustard, whisking to combine. Set aside.
10. Add the remaining oil to the pan and heat over medium-high heat. Add the apples and cook until they are soft, about 2 minutes, occasionally stirring gently. Remove the apples and set aside.
11. Add the onions and sage, stirring frequently until the onions are soft and begin to brown, about 5 minutes. Remove from the pan and set aside.
12. Deglaze the pan with the broth mixture, stirring to get everything off the bottom of the pan. Simmer the liquid until it has thickened and reduced by about half. Taste and adjust the seasoning if necessary.
13. Divide the rested chops among 4 plates. Top each with some of the apple-onion mixture, then spoon on the sauce.

Squirrel Piquante

*Sauce piquante (pronounced pee-*KAHNT*) is an extremely versatile Cajun sauce that can be used with any meat or seafood that you're lucky enough to catch—alligator, frog, crawfish, turtle, venison, or even just chicken. In fact, it's more like a stew or a gumbo than a sauce. When slow-cooked for hours, tougher meats like alligator, venison, or the squirrel used here become fork-tender, and the stew develops flavor and complexity.*

The French word piquante translates to "prickly," and in the context of food, it often means "spicy" or "zesty." While many a Cajun home would prepare this sauce to be quite hot, you can adjust the spice level to your own tastes. And always serve your sauce piquante with rice!

PREP TIME: 20 MINUTES   COOK TIME: 1 HOUR, 20 MINUTES   YIELDS: 4 SERVINGS

2 squirrels, field-dressed and cut into quarters
Salt and pepper
3 tablespoons olive oil
3 tablespoons flour
1 large sweet onion, minced
2 cloves garlic, minced
1 bell pepper, diced
3 tablespoons tomato paste
1 tablespoon Cajun seasoning (see Homemade Cajun Seasoning)
2 tablespoons Worcestershire sauce
One 28-ounce can crushed tomatoes
1 cup dry white wine
2 cups chicken broth
1 bay leaf

1. Season the squirrel generously with salt and pepper to taste.
2. Heat half the olive oil in a large saucepan or Dutch oven over medium heat. Add the meat of one squirrel, being sure not to overcrowd the pan.
3. Sear the meat until golden brown, about 2 minutes per side. Remove from pan and set aside. Repeat with the remaining squirrel.
4. Into the same pan, add the remaining 1½ tablespoons of oil and the flour. Stir constantly until the mixture is golden brown, about 1 minute.
5. Add the onions and soften for about 2 more minutes before adding the garlic and bell pepper. Stir the whole mixture occasionally and cook another 2 minutes.
6. Add the tomato paste and Cajun seasoning. Stirring constantly, cook for a minute.
7. Add the Worcestershire, tomatoes, wine, and broth. Whisk until smooth.
8. Add the bay leaf and browned squirrel.
9. Bring the mixture to a boil, then reduce heat to medium-low and simmer, stirring every 10 minutes, for at least an hour or until the squirrel meat is fork-tender.
10. Serve with rice.

Homemade Cajun Seasoning

Mix together 3 tablespoons of salt with 2 tablespoons each of garlic powder, oregano, and paprika. Add 1 tablespoon each of black pepper, cayenne, onion powder, and thyme. This makes a large batch that can be stored and used as needed. It's great with chicken, fish, or any other meat or seafood you'd like to give some Cajun flair.

MREs

Not all of us are as lucky as Rick and Michonne, when they found themselves falling into a storeroom filled with MREs (Meals, Ready-to-Eat) as they did in the Season 7 episode "Say Yes." These extremely shelf-stable meals were originally developed by the U.S. military as standard-issue field rations for soldiers. MREs are completely self-contained single-serving meals that can have shelf lives of up to ten years when stored in cool and dry conditions (though some have reported even longer spans), making them the gold standard in preserved foods and the ideal meal for the end of the world. After all, who among us can resist chili . . . and mac and cheese . . . together!

Sanctuary Seeded Bread

Who's got time to follow fussy bread recipes and knead dough when walkers are roaming the land? Not the survivors on The Walking Dead. *That's why this bread recipe couldn't be simpler. Mix together a few ingredients, let it sit overnight, and then bake. Not even toddler Judith Grimes could mess up this one.*

PREP TIME: 5 MINUTES   INACTIVE TIME: 8 TO 12 HOURS   COOK TIME: 1 HOUR
YIELDS: 4 SERVINGS

3 cups all-purpose flour
1 tablespoon kosher salt
1½ teaspoons instant yeast
1½ cups of warm water
1 cup oat bran
¼ cup pepitas
1 tablespoon black sesame seeds

1. Combine the flour, salt, and yeast in a large mixing bowl. Mix in the water. The dough should be scraggly and sticky.
2. Cover the bowl with plastic wrap and let it sit for 8 to 12 hours. The dough should be bubbly throughout.
3. Cover a baking tray with parchment paper, then sprinkle the oat bran, pepitas, and black sesame seeds over the surface. Dust your hands in flour to make handling the dough easier.
4. Punch the dough down in the bowl and scrape the sides down with your fingers to loosen it. Pick it up and quickly form it into a ball by pulling the outer edges down and in toward the center of the ball. Drop it onto the prepared parchment paper. Sprinkle the top liberally with flour, then loosely cover with plastic wrap or a clean kitchen towel.
5. Let it rest for half an hour. In the meantime, place a heavy ovenproof covered pot or dish (Dutch oven, Pyrex, or ceramic) in the oven. Preheat the oven to 450°F.
6. After the ball has rested for 30 minutes and the oven is preheated, carefully remove the hot pot from the oven.
7. Gently lifting the parchment, flip the bread into the pot, seam side up. Replace the cover and bake for 45 minutes.
8. Remove the cover and bake for another 15 minutes, or until deep golden brown.
9. Let the bread cool for 15 to 20 minutes before eating.

Adapted from Jim Lahey's recipe, originally published in the New York Times *in November 2006.*

Carl's Biscuits

When you fail to assassinate someone as unstable as Negan, the absolute best-case scenario is that you'll be forced to bake him biscuits and then share the most awkward dinner in the history of man. Though it might seem like for now Carl got off the hook far too easy after his ill-fated solo attack on the Sanctuary in Season 7's "Sing Me a Song," biscuit-making actually requires quite a bit of finesse, lest you end up with dense and chewy biscuits rather than light and buttery ones. Very cold butter is key, as is not overmixing the dough. And while some might say the secret ingredient in a perfect biscuit is love, with Negan breathing down Carl's neck, it was more likely hatred and contempt with just a sprinkle of terror for good measure.

PREP TIME: 10 MINUTES   COOK TIME: 15 MINUTES   YIELDS: 12 BISCUITS

3¾ cups flour
2 teaspoons salt
1 tablespoon baking powder
8 ounces unsalted butter, cut into small cubes and frozen
1½ cups buttermilk

1. Preheat the oven to 400°F. Line a baking tray with parchment paper.
2. In a large mixing bowl, whisk together the flour, salt, and baking powder.
3. Using a pastry blender or a fork, cut the butter into the flour until it resembles a coarse meal with pieces no larger than peas. Alternatively you could use a food processor and pulse the ingredients to achieve the same result. Transfer the mixture back to the bowl when you are done.
4. Mix in the buttermilk with a fork until just combined and a rough ball forms.
5. Turn the dough out onto a floured work surface. Gently pat it out into a rectangle. Fold the rectangle into thirds as you would a letter. Using a rolling pin, gently roll it out to about 1 inch thick.
6. Using a round cutter or a glass, cut the biscuits out by pressing firmly. Don't twist.
7. Put the biscuits onto the lined baking sheet, evenly spaced. Gently reroll any scraps.
8. Bake the biscuits for 13 to 15 minutes, until golden brown. Let them cool slightly before serving.

Simple Herb-Braised Rabbit

As much as he loves to feed his entire group for days by providing an entire deer, Daryl excels at trapping small game. While squirrel may be his specialty (see Squirrel Piquante—and let's face it, squirrel is much more abundant than deer—rabbit comes in a close second. Wild rabbit has a much deeper and more complex flavor than its farm-raised cousin, but both are fairly lean animals, and braising is an excellent way to keep their meat moist and tender.

To make the best use of all parts of the animal, make a stock from the bones and trimmings when you break down the rabbit. While this recipe uses some hard-to-scavenge items like white wine and Dijon mustard, the extra effort to find them will pay off in spades. You can also use your rabbit stock in place of the wine, or even substitute rabbit with a whole chicken if the local rabbits have managed to avoid your snares.

PREP TIME: 10 MINUTES   COOK TIME: 60 TO 75 MINUTES   YIELDS: 4 SERVINGS

1½ cups rabbit stock (see Making Rabbit Stock)
2 tablespoons Dijon mustard
2 tablespoons honey
2 cups dry white wine
2 tablespoons olive oil
Salt and pepper
½ cup flour
1 tablespoon tomato paste

1 whole rabbit (about 3½ pounds),
    broken down into 8 to 10 pieces
4 sprigs fresh rosemary
4 sprigs fresh sage
4 sprigs fresh thyme
1 bay leaf
4 cloves garlic, smashed but kept whole

1. Preheat the oven to 350°F.
2. In a medium mixing bowl, add the stock, Dijon mustard, honey, and wine. Whisk until combined and the honey has dissolved. Set aside.
3. Heat a large skillet with the olive oil over medium heat.
4. Pat the meat dry and season generously with salt and pepper, to taste.
5. Add the flour to a shallow baking dish. Dredge each piece of rabbit, shaking off the excess flour, and add it to the hot pan. Do not overcrowd the pan; divide the meat into two or more batches, as required.
6. Cook the rabbit until nicely browned on all sides, about 2 to 3 minutes per side. Remove the rabbit from the pan and set aside.
7. Add the tomato paste to the pan and stir constantly for 1 minute.

8. Pour 1 cup of the broth mixture into the pan and turn the heat up, scraping the bottom of the pan to get up all the browned bits. Pour this mixture into a 9-by-13-inch roasting pan or baking dish.
9. Transfer the rabbit to the roasting pan and cover with the remaining stock mixture. Scatter the fresh herbs and garlic into the dish. Cover the pan with foil. Braise for 50 minutes.
10. Uncover the pan and braise for an additional 10 to 15 minutes, or until the sauce reduces and thickens. Spoon juices over the rabbit every 5 to 10 minutes to keep it moist.
11. Transfer the rabbit pieces to a serving dish. Remove the sprigs of herbs and garlic cloves.
12. Pour the sauce over the rabbit. Serve with mashed potatoes.

Making Rabbit Stock

1. Heat a small pot with 1 tablespoon of oil over medium-high heat.
2. Brown all the trimmings from breaking down your rabbit.
3. When brown, add the bones you have trimmed.
4. Cover with 3 cups of water. Bring to a boil, then reduce heat and simmer for 30 minutes. Skim off any foam that might rise to the top.
5. Add a chopped carrot, celery stalk, half an onion, and a bay leaf. Simmer for another 2 hours.
6. Strain the liquid through a fine mesh strainer.
7. Return the stock to the heat to salt lightly, if desired. Otherwise, it's ready to use.

Roasted Garden Vegetable Medley

Even if your community's very best veggies have been claimed in the name of a villain like Negan, it's the fresh, herbaceous sauce that dresses this recipe that is the dish's true savior. A riff on the classic South American chimichurri sauce, this garlic-forward tangy sauce gets a little kick from the Governor's Pickled Peppers. Go ahead and use whatever garden veggies you have on hand and change it up as the seasons progress. Feel free to play with the herbs as well—oregano, cilantro, or mint would make great substitutes for the basil and tarragon.

PREP TIME: 10 MINUTES   COOK TIME: 20 TO 30 MINUTES   YIELDS: 4 SERVINGS

4 shallots, quartered
2 bell peppers, cut into large chunks
2 large zucchini, cut into ½-inch rounds
¼ cup plus 2 tablespoons olive oil, divided
1 teaspoon salt, divided
¼ teaspoon black pepper
¼ cup fresh tarragon
¼ cup fresh basil
¼ cup parsley
2 cloves garlic, sliced
1 tablespoon Governor's Pickled Peppers, minced
2 tablespoons lemon juice

1. Preheat the oven to 350°F. Line a large baking sheet with parchment paper.
2. Toss the vegetables with 2 tablespoons of the olive oil, ½ teaspoon of the salt, and the black pepper.
3. Roast the vegetables, stirring once, until tender and nicely browned, 20 to 30 minutes.
4. To the bowl of a food processor, add the tarragon, basil, parsley, peppers, and garlic. Pulse until no large pieces of garlic remain.
5. Add the remaining olive oil, the lemon juice, and the remaining salt. Pulse to combine. Transfer to a bowl and let sit until the vegetables are done.
6. Transfer the roasted vegetables to a large mixing bowl. Toss with ¾ of the dressing and let cool for 10 minutes.
7. Taste and, if necessary, adjust the seasoning. Serve with the remaining dressing drizzled on top.

Scalloped Potatoes from a Jar

It's fair to say that no one wants to cook after a long and arduous day of surviving in a world filled with the undead, so meals in a jar are a great way to save time, effort, and precious energy in any survival situation.

This recipe for creamy and satisfying scalloped potatoes will provide a little bit of shelf-stable comfort stashed away for when you need it and features entirely freeze-dried, dehydrated, or powdered ingredients. Sealed into a jar as is, the shelf life of this dish will be about a year. Add a couple of oxygen absorber packets (a staple for long-term food storage and readily available online) and you can double or triple the shelf life if you store the jars in cool, dry conditions. (See photo here for an example of the scalloped potatoes in the jar.)

PREP TIME: 20 MINUTES   COOK TIME: 35 TO 40 MINUTES   YIELDS: 4 SERVINGS

¼ cup powdered butter

¼ cup powdered milk

¼ cup powdered cheese

2 tablespoons flour

2 tablespoons cornstarch

1 teaspoon salt

½ teaspoon mustard powder

¼ teaspoon ground black pepper

½ cup freeze-dried mushrooms

½ cup freeze-dried asparagus

1 tablespoon dehydrated onions

3 cups dehydrated potato slices

½ tablespoon dehydrated chives

1 oxygen absorber

1. In a large bowl, mix together the butter, milk, cheese, flour, cornstarch, salt, mustard powder, and pepper. Pour the mixture into a quart jar.

2. Layer the mushrooms, asparagus, onions, and potato slices (in that order) on top of the powdered ingredients.

3. Put the chives into a small plastic baggie and tie to close. Place it on top of the vegetables.

4. Add an oxygen absorber. Seal the jar tightly and store in a cool, dry, and dark place until needed.

5. Preheat the oven to 350°F.

6. Remove the oxygen absorber and bag of chives. Carefully pour just the potatoes out of the jar and into a medium bowl.

7. Rehydrate by covering them with warm water for 15 to 20 minutes. Drain and pat dry.

8. Transfer the potatoes to a baking dish. Cover them with the remaining vegetables from the jar and mix gently to combine.

9. Pour the powdered ingredients into a large bowl, then add 2 cups of water and whisk until completely smooth.

10. Pour the liquid over the potatoes and vegetables. Sprinkle with the dried chives. Cover the dish tightly with foil.

11. Transfer to the oven and bake for 25 minutes.

12. Remove the foil and bake for an additional 10 to 15 minutes, until browned and bubbling. Let cool for 15 minutes before serving.

Chapter 4
Sweet Treats to Die For

Limiting your caloric intake will no longer be a concern if your world gets overrun with walkers, so if dessert is ever an option, indulging is the only acceptable answer. While an excess of sweets may not always be the best way to go for our favorite survivors—unless they've recently raided a dentist's office for a stockpile of toothpaste—enjoying some of life's simple edible pleasures could be just enough to get them through a long, hard day. And the extra added sugar rush might be enough to keep everyone alert and alive through the night as well!

Carl's Chocolate Pudding

Carl discovered that sometimes the best solution to what life throws at you is retreating to the rooftop and drowning his sorrows in an industrial-size can of chocolate pudding.

You can play with this recipe by substituting high quality cocoa powder and adding some espresso powder to give it a mocha flavor. But if you use the basics as outlined below you'll be pleasantly surprised that it will taste like it came right out of a can.

PREP TIME: 5 MINUTES, PLUS 4 HOURS
   FOR CHILLING
COOK TIME: 5 MINUTES
YIELDS: 4 SERVINGS

2 egg yolks
2 tablespoons cornstarch (3 tablespoons
   if eggs not available)
⅔ cups granulated sugar
2 cups whole milk, divided
¼ cup unsweetened cocoa powder
½ teaspoon kosher salt
1 teaspoon vanilla extract
1 tablespoon sweet butter

1. In a small bowl, whisk egg yolks until light and frothy, about 2 minutes. Whisk in the cornstarch and ½ cup of milk until dissolved, about 1 more minute. Transfer to a pourable measuring cup (like a Pyrex) and set aside.
2. In a medium saucepan, whisk together the sugar, remaining milk, cocoa powder, and salt over medium heat. Whisk constantly until the mixture starts to steam and little bubbles start to simmer around the edges, about 3 to 5 minutes.
3. Remove the cocoa mixture from the heat. Whisk in the egg yolk mixture in a very slow stream to avoid cooking the egg yolks.
4. Once fully incorporated, return to the heat and whisk constantly until the mixtures comes to a boil.
5. Reduce the heat to medium-low and keep whisking until the pudding is nice and thick.
6. Stir in the vanilla and butter. Transfer the pudding to a large bowl for chilling.
7. Put the bowl into the fridge uncovered. After 15 minutes, cover the bowl with plastic wrap, pushing the wrap into the surface of the pudding so no air remains. Chill for 4 hours or overnight. If you don't have access to a refrigerator, chill in the cold night air or pack ice or snow around the bowl.

Carol's Quarter Chocolate Bar Cookies

Surviving in a world like the one seen on The Walking Dead *doesn't often involve fresh-baked chocolate chip cookies, so once word gets out that a fresh batch is in the oven, expect to have all the local kids climbing through your window to get their hands on them.*

Since Carol stole more than her allotted quarter-bar of chocolate from Alexandria's freezer, it's only fitting that (despite its name) this recipe actually uses half a bar. The other secret ingredient in this recipe is applesauce, which makes a great egg replacement in baked goods. If you haven't scavenged any, make a batch of Aaron's Acceptable Applesauce.

These cookies make the perfect treat . . . or bribe, depending on who's seen you sneaking into the storeroom or weapons cache . . .

PREP TIME: 10 MINUTES   COOK TIME: 10 TO 12 MINUTES
YIELDS: 12 MEDIUM-SIZE COOKIES

¼ cup applesauce
¼ cup shortening
¼ cup brown sugar
¼ white sugar
¼ teaspoon vanilla
⅛ teaspoon salt
¼ teaspoon baking powder
¼ teaspoon baking soda
1 cup all-purpose flour
½ large (4-ounce) chocolate bar,
   chopped into large chunks

1. Preheat the oven to 350°F. Line two baking sheets with parchment.
2. In a medium bowl combine the applesauce, shortening, brown sugar, white sugar, and vanilla. Mix until well combined.
3. Add the salt, baking powder, baking soda, and flour. Mix until just combined. Set aside.
4. Melt the chopped chocolate in a double boiler, stirring until smooth.
5. Mix into the dough until fully blended.
6. Drop golf ball–size balls of dough onto the parchment-lined trays, about 2 inches apart.
7. Bake for 11 to 13 minutes, until set and lightly browned. Let cool slightly before serving.

Homemade Big Cat Bars

When Carl won what could have been the very last Big Cat bar on the planet in a friendly bet with Michonne in the Season 4 episode "Us," he gave half of it to her anyway. Some things just taste better when shared with someone we care about.

Vanilla sugar wafers, rice puffs, caramel, and chocolate all come together in the perfect harmony for this delectable homemade version. This recipe makes quite a few bars, but your supply won't last forever—so follow Carl's lead and be sure to share!

PREP TIME: 10 MINUTES   COOK TIME: 1 HOUR   YIELDS: 24 BARS

10 ounces soft caramels, unwrapped
2 tablespoons heavy cream
Dash of kosher salt
72 single-layer vanilla sugar wafer cookies
24 ounces bittersweet tempered chocolate melting discs, for dipping
1 cup puffed rice cereal

1. In a double boiler, melt the caramels with the cream and a dash of salt until smooth.
2. Remove from heat and allow the sauce to cool until it is thicker and less runny, about 15 minutes.
3. On a tray lined with parchment, arrange the wafers so they are evenly spaced.
4. Add a layer of caramel sauce to the top of each, spreading to cover the surface.
5. Top with another wafer, then spread a second layer of caramel.
6. Top with a third wafer. Don't worry if the caramel drips down the sides.
7. Put the tray into the fridge (1 hour) or freezer (30 minutes) to set.
8. In a double boiler, melt the chocolate until smooth, stirring occasionally.
9. Gently fold in the puffed rice cereal to the melted chocolate.
10. Dip each wafer sandwich into the chocolate and cover thoroughly (tongs and a spoon are useful for this). Return to the tray.
11. Allow to cool and set completely, about 2 hours or overnight.

Homemade Chocolate Clusters

Even though Eastman had rejected modern luxuries long before the world fell apart, one that he couldn't give up was chocolate. In "He's Not Here," he was often seen munching on candy and was even so kind as to share his personal stash while Morgan was under his care. These coveted confections became synonymous with the character, as evidenced by when Morgan left one precious packet on the altar of a church in memory of his dear, departed mentor. This recipe is inspired by those delicious confections.

PREP TIME: 4 HOURS, MOSTLY INACTIVE   COOK TIME: N/A   YIELDS: 12 CLUSTERS

2 tablespoons butter
½ cup sugar
1 tablespoon evaporated milk
2 cups mini marshmallows
One 8-ounce jar dulce de leche, chilled
2 cups salted peanuts
32 ounces bittersweet tempered chocolate melting discs, for dipping

1. Set up a baking tray lined with parchment paper.
2. Combine the butter, sugar, and evaporated milk in a small heavy-bottomed pot.
3. Melt on low until it just starts to bubble. Turn off the heat and let cool for 8 minutes.
4. Add the mini marshmallows and stir until the marshmallows are partially melted.
5. Scoop 12 mounds onto the parchment-lined tray and set in the freezer for 30 minutes.
6. Top each marshmallow mound with a scoop of cold dulce de leche, and then dip each mound's layer of dulce de leche into the salted peanuts, pressing lightly, and return it to the tray. Set in the freezer for another 20 minutes.
7. In a double boiler, melt the chocolate until smooth, stirring occasionally.
8. Using tongs, dip the bottom of each candy in the chocolate, and return it to the tray. Set in the freezer for 20 minutes.
9. Add a cooling rack to your parchment-covered tray. Put the clusters onto the cooling rack, then pour the remaining chocolate over each cluster to cover.
10. Let set completely for 2 hours or overnight.

Carol's Beet and Acorn Cookies

Leave it to Carol Peletier to demonstrate her kitchen wizardry by whipping up a unique batch of cookies from the limited resources available in Alexandria. With beets and flour made from foraged acorns, these unlikely delights boosted morale among her new neighbors and cemented her persona as the perfect homemaker. Much like the woman who baked them, though, these treats use their unexpected sweetness to hide what really lurks within.

PREP TIME: 15 MINUTES   COOK TIME: 14 TO 16 MINUTES   YIELDS: 24 COOKIES

1¼ cups all-purpose flour
¼ cup acorn flour
2 tablespoons plus 2 teaspoons
  arrowroot powder
1 teaspoon baking powder
1 teaspoon baking soda
½ teaspoon kosher salt

¼ cup canned beets, pureed
¼ cup canned water chestnuts, pureed
¼ cup canola oil
½ cup packed brown sugar
1 cup granulated sugar
1 teaspoon vanilla

1. Preheat the oven to 375°F. Line two baking sheets with parchment paper.
2. In a large mixing bowl whisk together the all-purpose flour, acorn flour, arrowroot powder, baking powder, baking soda, and salt. Set aside.
3. In another large mixing bowl, combine the pureed beets, pureed water chestnuts, canola oil, brown sugar, granulated sugar, and vanilla, whisking until well blended.
4. Add the dry ingredients to the wet, mixing until just incorporated.
5. Roughly divide the dough in half within the mixing bowl. Each half should make 12 cookies. Drop 12 heaping tablespoons of dough onto each of the baking trays.
6. Bake one tray at a time for 14 minutes, rotating the tray halfway through.
7. Bake for an additional 1 to 2 minutes if needed, until the cookies are set and slightly browned. Remove from the oven and cool completely.

Making Acorn Flour

Most varieties of oak produce acorns that are too bitter to eat, though generally white oaks produce sweeter and less tannic nuts than red oaks. You'll be able to distinguish white oaks from red because they have rounded rather than pointed leaves. Despite their bitterness, acorns are widely available all over North America and, with a little work, can become a valuable source of nutrition in survival situations. The most popular way to make use of acorn meat is by turning it into a meal, or flour. By grinding it up and leaching out the bitter tannins, you'll have a flour that can be used in a wide variety of recipes, including Carol's Beet and Acorn Cookies.

There are two ways you can go about doing this. You can blanch the meal in several changes of boiling water until it tastes good. This method is a lot faster, but it breaks down a starch in the flour that works a lot like gluten does in wheat flour, making it less useful in baking or as a thickening agent. Or, you can slowly leach the tannins out over the course of several days using cool or room-temperature water. This leaves the aforementioned starch intact and is the method outlined here.

Follow these steps to prepare your acorn flour:

1. Remove the outer shells from all nuts and soak them overnight. This will aid in peeling off the brown papery skin.
2. Drain and pat the nuts dry, then peel them.
3. Grind your acorns into fine meal using a mortar and pestle, or, if you have electricity, in a food processor.
4. Put the meal into a large bowl or other vessel that will allow you to cover it with enough water so that it's about half nuts, half water. Cover your vessel to keep critters out and store it in a cool (cooler than 75°F) dark place.
5. Each day, pour off the liquid, being careful not to pour out any meal. Test the meal—it's ready when it tastes bland, with no trace of bitterness. If it's not ready, refill the vessel with water. Stir vigorously.
6. Repeat as needed. The process can take anywhere from 5 to 14 days, depending on the acorn variety.
7. When the meal is ready, pour it through a strainer lined with cheesecloth or a coffee filter. Cheesecloth is preferable so you can tie it off and squeeze out all the excess moisture. If your cheesecloth seems flimsy, use several layers.
8. Spread the meal onto a baking tray to dry it out. You can do this in your oven at the lowest setting, with the door propped open. It's ready when it is completely dried, which could take several hours. Check it periodically and stir it so that it dries evenly.
9. Grind it further in a coffee grinder to get it to a flour consistency. Store it in the fridge or freezer, where it will last for a year or more.

Granny's Candied Pecans

We've seen many sides of Carol throughout the years—from timid and meek, to fierce and protective, to downright disturbing. But when she shelled foraged pecans with Lizzie and Mika and then lovingly roasted the nuts according to her grandmother's recipe in the Season 4 episode "The Grove," we got to see her show a rare maternal side.

Pecan trees are abundant in the South, and even if you can't go out and forage for their nuts in the wild like Carol did, you can forage through your local grocery store quite easily. These roasted, sweetened nuts are so addictive that you might assume that they are hard to make. Thankfully, the recipe is quick and easy, creating a great snack for long trips scavenging, scouting, or just looking at the flowers . . .

PREP TIME: 10 MINUTES   COOKING TIME: 5 MINUTES   YIELDS: 2 CUPS

3 tablespoons brown sugar
1 tablespoon water
¼ teaspoon vanilla
¼ teaspoon kosher salt
2 cups whole or halved pecans

1. Preheat the oven to 350°F.
2. Combine the brown sugar, water, vanilla, and salt in a small bowl and stir to combine. Set aside.
3. Spread the pecans in a single layer on a parchment-lined sheet tray. Toast in the oven until fragrant, about 5 minutes. Remove from the oven.
4. Transfer the pecans to a large saucepan and set the heat to medium.
5. Once the pan is hot, drizzle the glaze over the nuts, stirring constantly to coat well and prevent burning.
6. When the nuts are thoroughly coated, remove from the heat and immediately transfer them back to the parchment-lined tray, spreading them out so that they cool evenly.
7. Allow the nuts to cool to room temperature for about 2 hours, until hard and no longer sticky.
8. If needed, break them apart. Store them in an airtight container for up to a week.

Maggie's Forkless Apple Pies

Sometimes in life, doing good things earns you just desserts. So when the people of the Hilltop gave a fresh-baked apple pie to a pregnant Maggie as a thank-you for her heroic deeds in the Season 7 episode "Hearts Still Beating," it was no surprise that she bypassed the fork and devoured it with her bare hands before fellow survivors Sasha or Enid could even ask for a slice.

This variation is designed to be eaten utensil-free without leaving your trigger finger sticky in the process. Who has time for formalities such as table manners during the apocalypse anyway? A simple and easy way to enhance the apple flavor is to use a variety of apples—a mixture of sweet and tart, such as Golden Delicious and Granny Smith, for example, works very well.

PREP TIME: 1 HOUR COOK TIME: 25 MINUTES YIELDS: 8 SIX-INCH HAND PIES

Crust

2½ cups of all-purpose flour
1 tablespoon granulated sugar
1 teaspoon salt
1 cup (2 sticks, or ½ pound) butter,
  cubed and chilled
10 to 12 tablespoons ice water
1 egg, beaten with 1 tablespoon water, for washing
¼ cup coarse sugar crystals, for sprinkling

Filling

2½ cups apple, cored, quartered, and finely diced
1 tablespoon lemon juice
¼ cup granulated sugar
½ tablespoon flour
½ tablespoon cornstarch
1 pinch salt
¼ teaspoon cinnamon
1 pinch nutmeg
1 pinch ground allspice

1. Mix together the flour, sugar, and salt in a large mixing bowl.
2. Using a fork or pastry blender, incorporate the chilled butter until pea-size pieces of butter remain. Alternatively you can use a food processor and pulse the mixture until there are pea-size pieces of butter, then transfer the mixture to a large mixing bowl.
3. Working quickly, sprinkle 4 tablespoons of the ice water into the flour mixture and incorporate with a fork. Sprinkle in more water by the tablespoon and incorporate until the dough holds firmly together when pinched—if it crumbles apart when pinched, keep sprinkling.
4. When the dough firmly holds together, gently bring it together with your hands and then turn it out onto a floured surface. Fold it over itself a few times to bring it together, then cut it in half.
5. Shape each half into a ball. Flatten each ball into a disk, then roll each disk on its edge to smooth it out. Cover each disk in plastic wrap and refrigerate for 30 minutes.
6. Preheat the oven to 375°F. Line two baking sheets with parchment paper.
7. When the dough is chilled, combine all filling ingredients in a large mixing bowl and toss to coat evenly. Set aside.
8. Whisk together the egg and water for the egg wash. Set aside.
9. Leaving one disk in the fridge, roll out one disk to about ¼-inch thick. Using a round 6-inch cutter, cut out four 6-inch rounds. Set scraps aside to reroll. Brush half of each round lightly with egg wash.
10. Add two tablespoons of filling to the half with the egg wash, then fold over the other half, pressing the edge down to seal. Crimp the edges with a fork.
11. Brush the top of each pie lightly with egg wash. Make three small slits in the top of each and sprinkle with the coarse sugar.
12. Bake for 18 to 20 minutes, or until golden brown. While the first batch bakes, roll out the remaining dough and assemble another 4 pies.
13. Allow the pies to cool for 5 to 10 minutes before serving.

Georgia Peach Crumble

Georgia is known for its tempting, juicy peaches, which is why we've seen them pop up on the show. If it's not peach season, make use of apricots, plums, apples, or pears, or canned peaches from your survival stockpile!

PREP TIME: 10 MINUTES   COOK TIME: 50 MINUTES   YIELDS: 8 SERVINGS

6 cups sliced peaches (about 2 pounds)
1 cup plus two 2 tablespoons flour, divided
½ cup white sugar
1 teaspoon cinnamon
½ teaspoon nutmeg
¾ teaspoon salt, divided
3 tablespoons lemon juice, or apple cider vinegar
¼ cup packed brown sugar
6 tablespoons sweet butter, at room temperature

1. Preheat the oven to 350°F.
2. In a large mixing bowl, combine the sliced peaches, 2 tablespoons of the flour, the white sugar, cinnamon, nutmeg, ¼ teaspoon of the salt, and the lemon juice.
3. Toss until everything is well combined, then transfer to a large baking dish.
4. In another large mixing bowl, whisk together the brown sugar, the remaining 1 cup of flour, and the remaining ½ teaspoon of salt.
5. Add the butter and use your hands or a pastry blender to combine until large chunks form.
6. Cover the peaches with the crumble.
7. Bake until the center is bubbling, 40 to 50 minutes. Check after 30 minutes and cover with foil if sufficiently browned before it's bubbling.
8. Let it cool for 20 minutes before serving.

Foraged Berry Cobbler

There's no denying that the residents of the Kingdom love their cobbler. A savory version can become an epic meal (see The Kingdom's Breakfast Cobbler), but the classic dessert variety can make even the most down-on-their-luck survivor feel like postapocalyptic royalty.

No matter where you call home, chances are you can forage some wild berries. Some of the less commonly known varieties, such as juneberries and huckleberries, are entirely edible, but unless you know for sure what you're foraging or have a color field guide with you, avoid anything you can't identify with 100 percent certainty. Blackberries, raspberries, blueberries, and strawberries are all familiar berries you can find in the wild—if you know where to look. Berries generally grow low to the ground. Most berries enjoy full sun, so look for them at the edge of wooded areas, pastures, and fields, near sunny roadways, and along fences. The presence of birds and bees is a good sign that there might be berries nearby.

PREP TIME: 10 MINUTES   COOK TIME: 40 MINUTES   YIELDS: 4 TO 6 SERVINGS

Filling
5 cups fresh foraged berries, washed
½ cup sugar
2 teaspoons cornstarch
1 tablespoon lemon juice

Biscuits
1 cup all-purpose flour
1 teaspoon baking powder
1 teaspoon sugar
½ teaspoon salt
¼ cup butter, melted and cooled
½ cup buttermilk (reconstituted powdered buttermilk, if that's all
that's available)

1. Preheat the oven to 400°F.
2. In a large bowl, toss together all the filling ingredients.
3. Pour into a large baking dish. Set aside.
4. Whisk together the flour, baking powder, sugar, and salt.
5. Fold in the melted butter and buttermilk until just combined.
6. Pinch pieces of the dough onto the berry mixture. Don't worry if there are bald spots.
7. Bake until the biscuits are golden brown and the berries bubbling, 30 to 40 minutes.
8. Allow the cobbler to cool for 20 to 30 minutes before serving.

Sneaky Strawberry Pound Cake

When Beth found herself stuck at Grady Memorial under the watchful eye of former police officer Dawn Lerner in Season 5, she was forced to get a little sneaky. She bribed a fellow resident with deliciously ripe strawberries so that he would create a distraction while she stole medicine for Carol. This berry-based masterpiece honors Beth's boldness, and it may be just what the doctor ordered.

PREP TIME: 15 MINUTES   COOK TIME: 60 MINUTES   YIELDS: 8 TO 10 SERVINGS

12 ounces (3 sticks) unsalted butter, at room temperature,
   plus more for greasing the pans
3 cups all-purpose flour, plus more for dusting
2 teaspoons salt
2 teaspoons baking powder
3 cups plus ¼ cup granulated sugar, divided
6 large eggs, at room temperature
2 teaspoons vanilla extract
2 cups light sour cream or reconstituted powdered buttermilk
1 pound of fresh strawberries, sliced
1 tablespoon lemon zest
2 tablespoons lemon juice

1. Preheat the oven to 325°F. Butter two 9-by-5-inch loaf pans and dust with flour.
2. In a large mixing bowl, whisk together the flour, salt, and baking powder. Set aside.
3. In the bowl of an electric mixer, beat together the butter and 3 cups of sugar on a medium-high speed until very pale, light, and fluffy, about 8 minutes.
4. Scrape down the sides of the bowl before adding the eggs, one a time. Scrape down the bowl after each egg addition.
5. Add the vanilla. Reduce the mixing speed to low.
6. Add the flour in halves, alternating with the sour cream, until just incorporated. Don't overmix!
7. Split the batter between the two prepared loaf pans, using a spatula to smooth out the surface of the batter.
8. Bake on the middle rack of the oven until a cake tester comes out clean, 65 to 75 minutes.
9. In the meantime, toss together the strawberries with the remaining ¼ cup of sugar, the lemon zest, and the juice. Set aside until serving.
10. Let the cakes cool in their pans for about half an hour before turning them out and allowing them to cool completely.
11. Serve the cake in slices topped with the macerated strawberries.

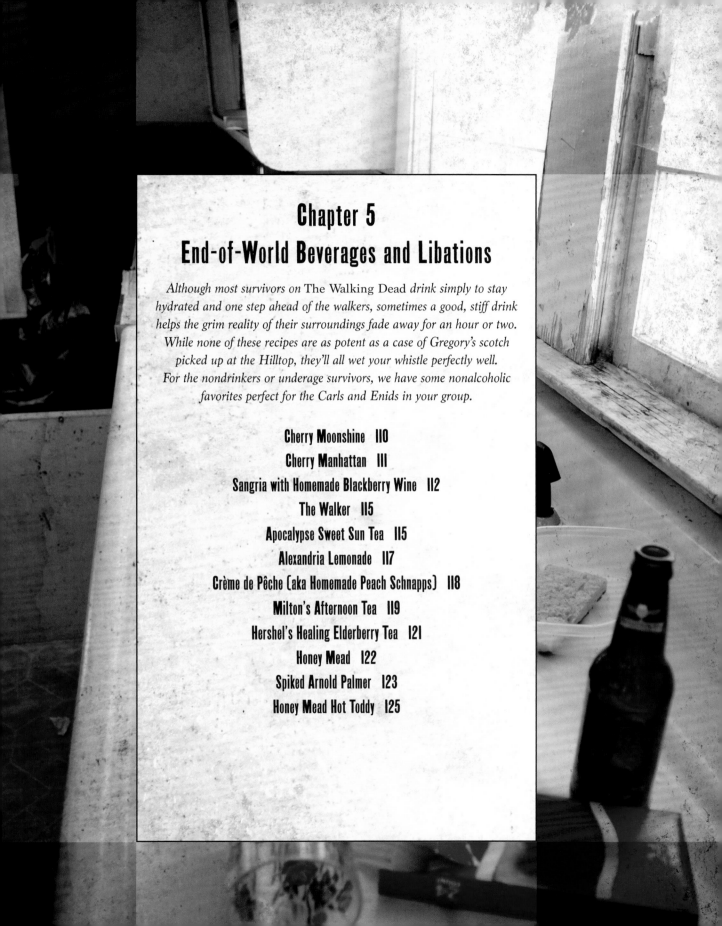

Chapter 5
End-of-World Beverages and Libations

Although most survivors on The Walking Dead *drink simply to stay
hydrated and one step ahead of the walkers, sometimes a good, stiff drink
helps the grim reality of their surroundings fade away for an hour or two.
While none of these recipes are as potent as a case of Gregory's scotch
picked up at the Hilltop, they'll all wet your whistle perfectly well.
For the nondrinkers or underage survivors, we have some nonalcoholic
favorites perfect for the Carls and Enids in your group.*

Cherry Moonshine

Having refused to let Beth drown her sorrows in sickly sweet peach liqueur, Daryl led her to a secret stash of moonshine instead, helping Beth and Daryl literally burn down some bad memories thanks to its highly flammable nature.

While distilling your own moonshine may not be practical, advisable, or perhaps even legal, this fun homage made with high-proof grain alcohol will be a warming, welcome addition to the Cherry Manhattan, and when packed into small mason jars, it makes a great gift for your favorite survivalists.

PREP TIME: 10 MINUTES   YIELDS: 10 CUPS

32 ounces tart cherry juice
One 30-ounce can tart cherries in syrup or water
¾ cup sugar
2¾ cups Everclear or other high-proof grain spirit

1. In a large saucepan over medium-low heat, gently heat the cherry juice, canned cherries, and sugar until the sugar is just dissolved. Don't boil it!
2. Remove from the heat and allow this mixture to cool completely before proceeding. This may take several hours but is an important step.
3. Combine the cooled cherry mixture and Everclear, mixing until incorporated.
4. Transfer to jars. The moonshine is ready to be used but will taste better if you let it sit for at least two weeks before consuming.
5. Store, sealed tightly, in a cool stream, an underground survival cache, or, if available, in the fridge.

Cherry Manhattan

Strong enough to wake the dead but delicious enough that you might not care, this cocktail makes use of Cherry Moonshine and will probably taste a heck of a lot better than anything you'd mix up in your bathtub. In dire survival situations when you can't get out to scavenge, combine 1 full ounce of moonshine with 2 ounces of bourbon and call it a day. But if you can manage to find vermouth and bitters, you can round this one out to make a proper Manhattan.

PREP TIME: 5 MINUTES   YIELDS: 1 COCKTAIL

2 ounces bourbon
½ ounce Cherry Moonshine
½ ounce sweet vermouth
2 dashes Angostura bitters
Cherry from the moonshine for garnish

1. Add the bourbon, moonshine, vermouth, and bitters to a mixing glass.
2. Add ice and stir until chilled, for 30 seconds.
3. Strain into a chilled cocktail glass.
4. Garnish with a cherry from the moonshine.

Sangria with Homemade Blackberry Wine

When all is quiet inside Alexandria's walls, sometimes there's nothing more to do than kick back on the porch with a drink and wait for the next impending disaster to arrive. While anticipating the worst, it wouldn't hurt them to indulge in the best that summertime has to offer—the delicious berry-infused flavors of this homemade sangria.

PREP TIME: 10 MINUTES   YIELDS: 4 TO 6 DRINKS

1 bottle dry white wine
1 cup homemade blackberry mead (see note below)
¼ cup simple syrup
Splash seltzer or club soda
Fresh blackberries for garnish
Mint for garnish

1. Combine the white wine, blackberry mead, and simple syrup in a large pitcher.
2. Refrigerate for at least 2 hours.
3. When serving, add the seltzer to taste and some ice to the pitcher.
4. Drop a couple of fresh berries into each glass before filling.
5. Garnish with a mint sprig.

TIP: To make the blackberry mead used in this recipe, just add 2 pounds of fresh blackberries to the Honey Mead recipe. Add the fruit along with the honey in Step 3, and then strain off the fruit before putting on the air lock. See below.

Making Meads and Fruit Wines

Mead is an ancient alcoholic beverage that's been enjoyed all over the world for millennia. The basic Honey Mead is a very versatile recipe, where you can add any single fruit or combination of fruits that you like—so experiment and have fun! As a general rule of thumb, use 2 to 3 pounds of fruit per gallon of liquid. The chlorine in munici-pally treated water can be harmful to the yeasts in mead, so use spring water when possible. And always use raw, unpasteurized honey, especially in basic honey meads, as it will be a source of wild yeast.

1. Mix Honey, Water, and Add-Ins
Add your water and honey to a wide-mouthed gallon jar or other clean vessel. Whisk vigorously until the honey has fully dissolved and the mixture is frothy and bubbly on the surface. Add whatever fruit you might be using and stir vigorously again for about a minute. Cover with cheesecloth or another clean breathable fabric, like a kitchen towel, and secure with string or a rubber band to keep critters out. Store in a cool, dark place like a cabinet.

2. Initial Ferment
Remove the cover and stir the mixture vigorously several times a day. The more the better! You are trying to aerate the mixture at this point, as this will help the growing yeast population. After a day or two, you will notice bubbles foaming up when you stir—this is a good sign! You will also start to smell a yeasty aroma, another good sign! The length of the initial ferment will vary depending on whether

you are using fruit and, if so, what kinds of fruit you use. It can happen in as little as a couple of days, so pay close attention. You will know the initial fermentation is done when the yeasty aroma has turned into a sweet and pleasant one. If using fruit, it's important to strain promptly at this stage because the fruit will begin to sour and affect the flavor of your mead. Don't toss the strained fruit! You can use this slightly fermented fruit in baking or eat it with oatmeal or yogurt. It's very tasty.

3. Second Ferment, with Air Lock
After the initial ferment, transfer the mead to a narrow-necked vessel like a carboy or growler. The vessel should be filled just up to the neck to minimize the oxygen exposure, so top it up if needed with additional honey and water (use a 4:1 ratio of water to honey). You will need air-lock tops for the vessels at this point because now we need to cut off the oxygen supply to our yeast population; otherwise you'll end up with vinegar! The air lock allows the gases created by fermentation to escape without oxygen getting in. If you prematurely close off the bottle with a screw top or other lid, the gas will have nowhere to escape to and you run the risk of your vessel exploding. You can improvise an air-lock lid with plastic tubing, as shown below, or even by using a balloon.

4. Rack the Mead
Check the mead periodically at this point, and look for the bubbling action within the liquid to stop completely. This should take anywhere from a few weeks to a few months. Now it is time to "rack" your mead, which means straining off the spent yeast that has settled at the bottom. Slowly pour the mead into a second vessel until you see a thicker and more opaque liquid, the lees, and stop. Throw away the lees. At this point you can drink the mead or let it ferment further to increase the alcohol content. If you want to ferment it further, transfer it back to your narrow-necked vessel. Top up with 4:1 water-and-honey mixture as needed. This whole process will have kicked up another bout of bubbling, and once this has subsided (again, a few weeks to a few months) your brew will have fermented "to dryness," which means that all available sugars have been turned into alcohol. Taste the mead. If you like it, you can drink it. If you're less than enthused, age it. Aging often improves the flavor of meads considerably!

5. Age the Mead
To age your mead, transfer it to smaller bottles (bail-top bottles are great for this) and seal with lids or corks. Be sure the fermentation is done before aging—if you seal off the bottles prematurely, you run the risk that the contents will explode. If you can, lay the bottles on their sides for a more even aging process. Age anywhere from six months to a year, tasting periodically.

The Walker

This cocktail (pictured left) is equally great for both the fall season and the fall of civilization. It's also seriously boozy beneath its deceptively mellow surface. Be warned: Too many of these and you'll be stumbling around like a walker—which, in the world of The Walking Dead, *might greatly increase your odds of actually becoming one. Either way, drink responsibly!*

PREP TIME: 5 MINUTES   YIELDS: 1 COCKTAIL

1½ ounces bourbon
1½ ounces Honey Mead
1 ounce fresh apple cider, or juice if not available
2 dashes Angostura bitters
Nutmeg, freshly grated, for garnish

1. Add the bourbon, mead, apple cider, and bitters to a shaker.
2. Fill with ice, cover, and shake well, about 20 seconds.
3. Strain over ice into a chilled rocks glass and garnish with freshly grated nutmeg.

Apocalypse Sweet Sun Tea

Sweet tea is a household staple in the South. It's usually made in large batches so that it is always on hand in the fridge, and it's likely that the Greene family was never without a full pitcher. When the electricity and gas have been shut off and there's no fire handy to boil the water, feel free to let the sun do some of the hard work instead.

This is a traditional sweet tea with an apocalyptic flare. Using the power of the sun, you can steep black tea and then sweeten it with honey. You can easily adapt this recipe and steep the tea the traditional way, using boiling water— just cut the steep time down to five minutes. And feel free to play with the tea! Though the base of traditional sweet tea is plain black tea, you can add other black, green, or herbal teas to change the flavor profile.

PREP TIME: 5 HOURS   YIELDS: 1 GALLON

14 black tea bags
1 gallon water
1 cup honey
Fresh mint for garnish

1. Add the tea bags and water to a clean gallon jar and cover.
2. Place in direct sunlight for about 5 hours.
3. Add the honey and mix well until fully dissolved.
4. If you have a fridge available, chill in the fridge for 3 to 5 hours, or overnight.
5. Serve on ice with fresh mint sprigs, if they're available.

Alexandria Lemonade

Life may have handed our favorite survivors an endless supply of lemons, yet the residents of Alexandria still had to rely on powdered lemonade to quench Negan's thirst in the Season 7 episodes "Sing Me a Song" and "Hearts Still Beating." Sometimes, you have to make do with what you have, but if you're in a region where citrus is readily available, nothing beats homemade lemonade using fresh lemon juice.

You can stop after you've made the base (Step 5) and store it in the fridge, mixing with water as needed. Try adding some sparkling water for a refreshing fizzy lemonade, or use the original recipe as part of the Spiked Arnold Palmer.

PREP TIME: 5 MINUTES   COOK TIME: 5 MINUTES
YIELDS: 10 CUPS BASE, FOR ABOUT 20 CUPS LEMONADE

2 cups granulated sugar
2 cups water, plus more for diluting the base
3 cups freshly squeezed lemon juice (2 dozen lemons)
Fresh mint for garnish
Sliced lemon for garnish

1. Add the sugar to 2 cups of water in a medium saucepan over high heat.
2. Bring to a light boil and continue to cook until the sugar is completely dissolved.
3. Remove from the heat. Allow to cool completely before using.
4. In the meantime, juice all the lemons. Strain the juice through a fine mesh strainer to remove the pulp, if desired.
5. Add the cooled simple syrup to the fresh lemon juice. This is your lemonade base, and you can make lemonade with roughly 1 part base to 2 parts water, or to taste.
6. Fill a jug or individual glasses with ice. Add base and water (sparkling or still!). Garnish with fresh mint and lemon slices.

Crème de Pêche (aka Homemade Peach Schnapps)

When Beth just couldn't fathom another day on the run and was lamenting her previous normal life, she decided to just give in and have a drink in the Season 4 episode "Still." Grabbing any random bottle from behind a bar, she was perfectly content to make peach schnapps her first drink ever. Fortunately, Daryl was there to put his foot down.

This homemade peach liqueur (aka crème de pêche) might have changed Daryl's tune, though. Made with summer-ripened peaches, this is a fragrant and delicious addition to cocktails (like the Spiked Arnold Palmer) that can be drizzled over vanilla ice cream or even just enjoyed as a sipper on the rocks.

PREP TIME: ABOUT A WEEK   YIELDS: 4½ CUPS

8 large ripe peaches, sliced
One 750-ml bottle vodka
1 cup granulated sugar
1½ cups water

1. Combine the peaches and vodka in a large jar or glass bowl.
2. Let steep until the vodka is infused with peach flavor, up to a week.
3. In a small saucepan, bring the water and sugar to a boil.
4. Remove from the heat and allow to cool completely.
5. Combine with the peach vodka.
6. Store in the fridge.

Milton's Afternoon Tea

Not only was Milton Mamet a trusted advisor of the Governor with the responsibility of monitoring all activity in Woodbury, he was also tasked with performing experiments on walkers in an attempt to better understand them. So, it's understandable that Milton needed a break for tea every now and again. This fairly traditional English afternoon tea is a comforting way of taking a hard-earned respite from either the stress of everyday life or the demands of postapocalyptic living.

PREP TIME: 10 MINUTES   YIELDS: 4 CUPS

4 teaspoons loose-leaf black tea
4 cups water
½ cup milk
4 sugar cubes

1. Fill a teapot with hot tap water and wrap it with a tea towel. Set aside.
2. Bring 4 cups of water to a boil in a stovetop kettle, a medium saucepan, or an electric kettle.
3. Warm the milk in a small saucepan on the stove until steaming.
4. Pour out the hot water from the teapot and add the loose leaves.
5. Fill the pot with the boiled water, cover with the tea towel, and steep for 5 minutes.
6. Transfer the warm milk to a creamer, and put the sugar cubes into a small bowl.
7. Using a tea strainer, pour and serve the 4 cups sequentially.
8. Pass the milk and sugar around so that each person may adjust their tea to taste.

Hershel's Healing Elderberry Tea

When the survivors living in the prison suffered an outbreak of a mysterious virus, Hershel harnessed the power of Mother Nature and foraged for elderberries to make an immune system–boosting tea. Elderberries are high in vitamin C and are often used to fight off colds and flu. Commercially sold elderberry syrups have become quite popular over the past few years, and they can often be found alongside cold remedies in pharmacies. Foragers will also often make syrups and jams from the berries.

If you do forage for elderberries, be sure to discard all leaves, stems, and branches—they're poisonous. Only the flowers and berries are edible (and the berries should not be consumed raw). Elderberries are in season from July through August and can be found throughout Central Europe and North America, both in the wild and in most health food stores.

PREP TIME: 30 MINUTES   YIELDS: 4 CUPS

4 tablespoons dried elderberries
4 cups water
1 cinnamon stick
2 whole cloves
3 teaspoons raw honey

1. Add all ingredients except for the honey to a medium saucepan.
2. Bring to a boil, then reduce the heat and simmer for 30 minutes.
3. Strain off the berries and spices. Mix in the honey. Divide among 4 cups.

Honey Mead

Mead is a drink the Ancient Greeks wisely referred to as the nectar of the gods. Classic mead is nothing more than a fermented beverage of honey and water. Fruits, spices, and other flavorings can be added, but at its core it is simply honey and water, and it's dead easy to make (see Making Meads and Fruit Wines). Make sure the honey you use is raw and unpasteurized, and throw in a handful of raisins to help boost the lactic acid bacteria needed for fermentation.

PREP TIME: 6 TO 12 MONTHS, MOSTLY INACTIVE   YIELDS: 1 GALLON OF MEAD

1 gallon water, preferable spring
2½ pounds raw unpasteurized honey
1 handful raisins

1. Wash the vessel you will be using thoroughly. A glass gallon jar or ceramic crock are ideal, but you can also use food-safe plastic.
2. If using tap water, let it sit out overnight to evaporate the chlorine, which can kill yeast.
3. Add the water and honey to your vessel. Whisk vigorously until the honey is completely dissolved.
4. Add the handful of raisins.
5. Cover with cheesecloth and secure with an elastic band to keep out any unwanted critters. Store in a dark place.
6. Stir the mead vigorously several times a day. When it has attracted enough wild yeast it will start to bubble and fizz, and you should detect a yeasty aroma. Keep stirring several times daily until this bubbling and fizzing has subsided and a sweet aroma remains.
7. Transfer the mixture to a clean narrow-necked vessel like a carboy or growler. Cover the vessel with an air-locking top (see Making Meads and Fruit Wines). The key is to allow gases to escape but not let outside air in.
8. Check occasionally until the thick sediment of expended yeast (lees) has settled to the bottom and the mead appears to be fairly still (no bubbling), anywhere from nine to twelve months. You can drink the mead now or rack it for aging.
9. Pour off the mead carefully, leaving the lees in the bottom of the vessel.
10. Put the mead into smaller bottles, like wine bottles or E.Z. Cap beer bottles. Lay bottles on their sides to promote more even aging. Age for about six months before sampling.

TIP: To make the blackberry mead used in Sangria with Homemade Blackberry Wine, just add 2 pounds of fresh blackberries to this recipe. Add the fruit along with the honey in Step 3, and then strain off the fruit before putting on the air lock. See Making Meads and Fruit Wines.

Spiked Arnold Palmer

Beth's schnapps incident took place while she and Daryl were scavenging in an abandoned country club. Any golfer knows she would have been better off relaxing with the classic lemonade and iced tea hybrid known as an Arnold Palmer . . . though in her situation, no one would have blamed her for adding just a hint of booze to punch it up a notch. This play on that classic is a real hole in one, using the Alexandria Lemonade, the Apocalypse Sweet Sun Tea, and the homemade Crème de Pêche.

PREP TIME: 5 MINUTES   YIELDS: 1 DRINK

2 ounces Apocalypse Sweet Sun Tea
2 ounces Alexandria Lemonade
3 ounces Crème de Pêche
2 dashes Peychaud's bitters
2 ounces seltzer
Lemon slices for garnish

1. Add the tea, lemonade, schnapps, and bitters to a cocktail shaker with ice.
2. Shake vigorously for about 20 seconds.
3. Strain into a collins glass filled with ice, then top with seltzer.
4. Garnish with a lemon slice.

Honey Mead Hot Toddy

Not only does Honey Mead taste great, but it's an excellent bargaining chip, too. Other survivors who want to drink but aren't willing to put in the work will gladly trade crates of supplies for a barrel of mead . . . except, perhaps, Negan's henchman Simon. He's more of a tequila man. A hectic life of farming, trading, and keeping peace in a community is bound to wear down any survivor, though, so be sure to save some mead for yourself to make a nice hot toddy from time to time.

Toddies are known for their warming and restorative properties, and they have been used as a cold and flu remedy for centuries. You'll get vitamin C boost from the lemon, a soothing effect from the honey, and just enough numbing from the booze to make even Rick forget that the Saviors are knocking on his door.

PREP TIME: 5 MINUTES   YIELDS: 1 DRINK

2 ounces bourbon
1½ ounces Honey Mead
½ ounce maple syrup
½ ounce lemon juice
2 dashes Angostura bitters
8 ounces hot water
1 cinnamon stick
Lemon slice for garnish

1. Add the bourbon, mead, maple syrup, lemon juice, and bitters to a large mug.
2. Top with hot water, using the cinnamon stick to stir until well combined.
3. Float the lemon slice on top for garnish.

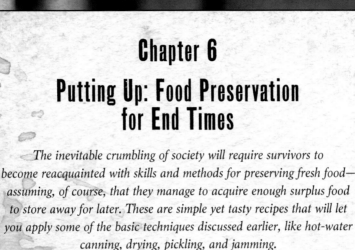

Chapter 6
Putting Up: Food Preservation for End Times

The inevitable crumbling of society will require survivors to become reacquainted with skills and methods for preserving fresh food—assuming, of course, that they manage to acquire enough surplus food to store away for later. These are simple yet tasty recipes that will let you apply some of the basic techniques discussed earlier, like hot-water canning, drying, pickling, and jamming.

DIY Deer Jerky

Jerky is a staple foodstuff and one of the most reliable ways to preserve extra meat that you just can't scarf down in a few servings. Any meat you're fortunate enough to find can likely be turned into jerky, as the residents of Terminus know. Jerky makes a great high-protein take-along snack for hunting trips, scavenging missions, and even on those long journeys to distant communities and places unknown.

Feel free to adjust the seasonings in your brine to taste, as this is where most of the flavor will come from. This recipe also calls for liquid smoke and makes use of an oven, but the true survivor can use a smoke tepee to add a smoky flavor and aid in sun-drying.

PREP TIME: 14 HOURS, MOSTLY INACTIVE   COOK TIME: 5 TO 8 HOURS   YIELDS: 1 POUND

4 pounds lean deer meat, preferably the eye
   round and rump roast cuts, trimmed of fat
   and silverskin
¾ cup Worcestershire sauce
¾ cup soy sauce
1 teaspoon garlic powder
1 teaspoon onion powder

1 teaspoon chile flakes
2 tablespoons molasses
1 tablespoon honey
½ teaspoon curing salt,
   or follow package directions
2 teaspoons liquid smoke

1. Freeze the meat for about an hour or two before slicing—this will help you get more consistent cuts. Cutting against the grain of the meat, make your slices about ⅛ of an inch thick.
2. Whisk together the Worcestershire, soy sauce, garlic and onion powders, chile flakes, molasses, honey, curing salt, and liquid smoke in a large bowl.
3. Put the sliced meat in a large resealable plastic bag and pour the marinade into the bag. Push out as much air as possible and seal.
4. Marinate the meat for 12 hours in the fridge.
5. Preheat your oven to 175°F. Line two baking sheets with parchment and place cooling racks on them.
6. Remove the strips of meat from the marinade and lay them out on the cooling racks, letting them drip dry for 20 to 30 minutes.
7. Transfer the trays to the oven. Dry the meat until it cracks deeply when you bend it and feels dried through to the touch, anywhere from 5 to 8 hours, depending on your oven.
8. Store in an airtight container. The jerky will keep for at least three months.

Building a Smoke Tepee

A smoke tepee could be quite useful when Daryl brings home a surplus of meat and you are without an oven or electricity. It's used as an aid for sun-drying meats, as opposed to using the fire and smoke to cook or otherwise dry out the meat. (For more on sun-drying foods, see our "Food Preservation" guide.) A smoldering fire—a fire burned down to embers—is built at the base of the tepee to deter flies and other pests from the meat while it is drying in the sun.

Be sure to use hardwoods (maple, oak, beech, etc.) rather than softwoods (pine, fir, cedar, spruce). Softwoods tend to burn faster and smokier than hardwoods, and they will give food a rancid flavor.

To construct a smoking tepee, make a tripod by binding together three large 6-foot sticks near their tops, using rope or another sturdy binder like twine. Create racks by binding sticks between the three poles. The racks should sit about 3 feet from the ground. Be sure to move your tepee throughout the day so that it stays in direct sunlight.

Once the meat is thoroughly dried on the surface, insects and other pests should leave it alone, and you can finish drying it without the smoke. Too much smoke will give your jerky a bitter, rancid flavor.

Aaron's Acceptable Applesauce

In Season 5, after Aaron approached Rick and his group with an invitation to join Alexandria, he initially stoked their suspicions when he refused to eat a jar of applesauce he was carrying, leading Rick to believe it might be poisoned. The truth was that Aaron simply couldn't stomach the stuff due to a bad childhood experience. Too bad for Aaron, because applesauce is a perfect food for postapocalyptic living.

Besides being easy to make and a great way of preserving fall apples for the winter and spring, it works as a great accompaniment to meats, pairing especially well with pork and wild boar. You can also use it as a fat or egg replacement in baked goods of all kinds—cookies, cakes, loaves, pancakes, waffles, muffins, and more.

PREP TIME: 30 MINUTES　　　　COOK TIME: 20 MINUTES　　　　YIELDS: 2 QUARTS

7 pounds apples, peeled, cored, and cut into 2-inch pieces
One 2-inch cinnamon stick
¼ cup water
¼ cup honey
2 tablespoons lemon juice or apple cider vinegar

1. Prepare the canning equipment (see "Food Preservation" guide).
2. Add the apples, cinnamon stick, and ¼ cup of water to a large saucepan over medium heat.
3. When the water starts to simmer, partially cover and cook for 15 to 20 minutes, or until the apples are soft and cooked through. The cooking time will vary depending on the variety of apple; avoid overcooking by checking the doneness frequently.
4. Remove from heat and mash the apples until they reach the desired consistency.
5. Return the pot to a medium-high flame, stirring in the honey and acid.
6. Bring to a boil, then reduce the heat to low in order to keep the applesauce warm while transferring it to jars.
7. Ladle the sauce into your prepared jars, leaving ½ inch of headspace. Wipe the rims if necessary, put on the lids, and screw on the bands until tight.
8. Submerge the jars in your canner and process for 20 minutes.
9. Turn off the heat and let sit for 5 minutes before removing to cool completely.
10. After 24 hours, check to make sure the jars have sealed correctly. The applesauce can be stored in a cool dry place for at least a year.

Grady Memorial Dried Fruit Trail Mix

Grady Memorial Hospital's impressive rooftop farm was fully loaded with container plants and huge drying trays covered in fruits and vegetables.

Sun-drying fruits and vegetables is fairly easy, and if you have the right climate (cool, sunny, and dry), it is an almost effortless way to preserve foods for the winter (see "Food Preservation" guide). You can use a mix of whatever fruits and nuts you like, but for an extra apocalyptic challenge, try foraging and processing your own nuts. Roasting your nuts and seasoning them with salt creates a salty-sweet trail mix, but you can skip the salt if you like.

PREP TIME: ABOUT A WEEK, WEATHER PERMITTING
COOK TIME: 5 TO 10 MINUTES
YIELDS: 1 POUND

2 pounds seasonal fruit, such as apple or pear
8 ounces mixed foraged nuts, such as pecans or walnuts
1 tablespoon canola oil
Kosher salt

1. Peel, core, and slice your fruit.
2. Sun-dry the fruit (see "Food Preservation" guide).
3. Once the fruit is completely dried and pasteurized, dice it into bite-size pieces similar in size to the nuts in your mix.
4. Preheat the oven to 350°F.
5. In a large bowl, toss the nuts with the canola oil. Add salt to taste.
6. Spread the nuts out in a single layer on a parchment-lined tray and roast until fragrant and lightly browned, about 5 to 10 minutes.
7. Remove from oven and let them cool completely before continuing, at least 2 hours or overnight.
8. Mix together the dried fruit and roasted nuts.
9. Store in an airtight container or resealable food storage bag.

The Governor's Pickled Peppers

Before the fall of Woodbury, the Governor seemed to be the king of his dark, twisted world. He had cushy quarters, a supply of whiskey, a full detail of dedicated henchmen, and a verdant backyard oasis teeming with fresh hot peppers. If he hadn't been so concerned with pickling those walker heads he kept in his aquariums, perhaps he would have thought to preserve some of those peppers . . .

Pickled hot peppers can add a spicy little kick to anything from pizzas to pastas, hot dogs to grilled cheese, dips, and hors d'oeuvres. Chop a few up and fold them into the Governor's Welcome Scramble or use them in the sauce for the Roasted Garden Vegetable Medley.

Always wear rubber gloves when handling hot peppers. Without them, it's far too easy to later rub your eye and accidentally incur the burning wrath of the pepper's oils. This is particularly troublesome if you have just the one eye . . .

PREP TIME: 30 MINUTES PLUS 2 WEEKS   COOK TIME: 30 MINUTES   YIELDS: 1 QUART

2 cups white vinegar
⅔ cups water
2 tablespoons kosher salt
2 tablespoons sugar
½ teaspoon black peppercorns
1 teaspoon coriander seeds
½ teaspoon mustard seeds
4 cups (about 1 pound) assorted hot peppers,
   sliced or chopped according to preference
2 cloves garlic, gently crushed

1. Prepare your canning bath and jars
   (see "Food Preservation" guide).
2. In a medium saucepan, bring all ingredients
   save for the peppers and garlic to a boil.
3. Reduce heat and simmer for 5 minutes.
4. While the brine simmers, pack two prepared
   pint-size or one prepared quart-size jar with
   the peppers and garlic.
5. Pour the hot brine into the jar(s), leaving
   about ½ inch of headspace.
6. Put on the lids and secure with the metal
   bands until tight. Put the jar(s) into your
   hot-water bath and bring to a boil. Process
   for 20 minutes.
7. Turn off the heat and let sit for 5 minutes
   before removing and allowing to cool completely
   overnight.
8. Inspect each jar to ensure it has sealed
   properly. Let the peppers pickle for two weeks
   before eating.

Fruit and Veggie Leathers

Not only is fruit leather a sneaky way to get kids to eat fruit, it's also an excellent way to preserve fruits and vegetables—a shelf-stable snack that comes in handy for survivors when they're trekking the wasteland or on a long shift in the Alexandria watchtower. Though generally associated with fruit, adding vegetables like spinach or kale will boost nutrition without taking away from flavor.

As a rule of thumb, about two cups of fresh fruit are needed for a 13-by-15-inch tray. This recipe calls for strawberries and spinach, but play around with combinations—strawberries and beets, apples and spinach, raspberry and kale—whatever is in season or on hand from your prison farm or rooftop garden. Be sure to spread the mixture as evenly as possible. An offset spatula or the flat side of a katana can be great tools!

PREP TIME: 15 MINUTES   COOK TIME: 5 TO 8 HOURS   YIELDS: 6 ROLL-UPS

2½ cups fresh strawberries, hulled
½ cup packed fresh spinach
¼ cup honey
2 teaspoons lemon juice or apple cider vinegar

1. In a blender or food processor, process the strawberries, spinach, and honey until very smooth. If the mixture seems thick, add water or some of Aaron's Acceptable Applesauce in tablespoon increments to thin it until it pours easily.
2. Stir in the lemon juice.
3. Preheat the oven to 175°F.
4. Pour the mixture into the middle of a parchment-lined baking tray. Using a spatula (or an offset spatula, if you have one), spread the puree into a thin layer, making it as even as you possibly can.
5. Dry the leather in the oven until the center is firm and no longer sticky, anywhere from 5 to 8 hours.
6. Remove from the oven and allow to cool completely.
7. Remove the leather from the baking tray and, keeping the parchment intact, cut the sheet into thirds, and then cut each third into halves.
8. Form each strip into a narrow roll. The leather will last about a month at room temperature, or about a year properly packaged in the freezer.

Carriage Bar Pickled Eggs

Pickled eggs are a great bar snack and an excellent way of putting up a precious commodity like protein during lean times. Their creamy centers, paired with savory aromatics such as garlic, dill, and caraway, make these eggs addictive and would have made a nice alternative to liquor when Rick and Hershel had their heart-to-heart about Hershel's pas' drinking problems at the Carriage Bar in the Season 2 episode "Nebraska."

You can change up the aromatics according to taste and availability: diced onion, juniper berries, whole allspice, mustard seeds, bay leaves, and cinnamon sticks are all popular additions for pickling brines.

PREP TIME: 10 MINUTES PLUS 1 WEEK FOR PICKLING
COOK TIME: 1 HOUR
YIELDS: 24 EGGS

2 dozen eggs
1 large sprig dill, or two smaller sprigs
1 clove garlic, sliced
1 jalapeño, sliced
3 cups white vinegar
1 cup water
1 cup sugar
2 tablespoons kosher salt
½ teaspoon peppercorns
½ teaspoon caraway seeds

1. Add the eggs to a large saucepan, cover with water, and bring to a boil over high heat.
2. Turn off the heat, cover the pot, and let the eggs sit for 5 minutes. In the meantime, prepare an ice bath.
3. After 5 minutes have passed, transfer the eggs to the ice bath using a slotted spoon. Let them sit for another 5 minutes. This will make peeling them much easier.
4. After carefully peeling each egg, gently return it to the ice bath to rinse off any remaining bits of shell while you peel the rest.
5. Carefully place the eggs into a prepared half-gallon jar (see "Food Preservation" guide for information on preparing jars for canning). Add the dill, garlic, and jalapeño.
6. In a medium saucepan, bring the vinegar, water, sugar, salt, peppercorns, and caraway seeds to a boil over high heat, then reduce the heat and simmer for 5 minutes.
7. Remove from heat and let cool for 15 minutes.
8. Once the mixture has cooled, add it to the jar—there should be no more than about ½ inch of headspace at the top of the jar. Cover and let the jar sit to cool completely overnight.
9. Transfer the jar to the fridge. Wait at least a week before enjoying. The eggs will last indefinitely in the fridge.

Ms. So-and-So's Rhubarb Preserves

When Maggie and Sasha saved the Hilltop from an onslaught of walkers in the middle of the night the community's leader, Gregory, showed his gratitude by offering them some rhubarb preserves before attempting to send them on their way. In typical Gregory fashion, he couldn't even remember the name of the kind citizen who had made this delicious spread.

Rhubarb is one of the first signs of spring, as well as a great vegetable to preserve for cooler months, when fare gets heartier and heavier. The addition of rosemary makes this already versatile preserve even more so. You can go savory or sweet: It's a great accompaniment to meats or can be slathered on scones or Carl's Biscuits with fresh butter.

PREP TIME: 5 MINUTES   COOK TIME: 30 MINUTES   YIELDS: 1½ PINTS

4 cups rhubarb, chopped
1 cup honey or sugar
¼ cup water
1 sprig rosemary

1. Combine all ingredients in a medium saucepan. Over medium heat, stir frequently until the sugar dissolves. Cook until the rhubarb begins to fall apart and the mixture is nice and thick.
2. While the compote simmers, prepare the hot-water bath and jars for canning (see "Food Preservation" guide).
3. Remove the sprig of rosemary. Pour the hot compote into the jar(s), leaving about ½ inch of headspace.
4. Put on the lids and secure with the metal bands until tight. Put the jar(s) into your hot-water bath and bring to a boil. Process for 10 minutes.
5. Turn off the heat and let sit for 5 minutes before removing and allowing to cool completely overnight.
6. Inspect each jar to ensure that it has sealed properly. The jars can be stored in a cool, dark place for at least a year.

FINAL WORDS

As Rick and his fellow survivors on *The Walking Dead* have shown us, staying alive and well fed in a walker-infested world is not for the misinformed. It requires survival smarts, resourcefulness, and nerve to nourish your body and spirit when food and supplies are scarce. Luckily, you're now armed with this collection of tips and recipes to make postapocalyptic life a bit easier—and hopefully more delicious!

Whether growing food behind safe walls, hunting for it through unknown terrain, drying it in the open air, or preserving it in jars, the same principle applies: Preparedness is the key to survival. Also, no one likes to eat alone. Start preparing now by gathering your closest friends to make the tasty recipes in this book. It'll guarantee a solid team of compatriots on your side if the unimaginable ever happens. Best of luck!

ACKNOWLEDGMENTS

This book would not be possible without the talent, wisdom, experience, kindness, and support of so many people. First and foremost, thank you to the creators of the original *The Walking Dead* comic book, and thank you to AMC for bringing it to the screen. Thank you to all the writers, cast, and crew of the show for bringing this rich universe to life.

Thank you to my inspirations and compatriots in food at Rose's Bklyn, chef Buzz Frazier, Alicia Nicolette, and Kate O'Connor Morris, for helping me get my hands on a variety of critters for recipe-testing and for being generally wonderful humans. Thank you to Joe, Mike, Zoe, Phil, and Nad for being guinea pigs (not the kind found at Grady Memorial, mind you) during recipe-testing and for your endless love and support. Thank you to Alex Middleton of Zero Feet Per Second for teaching me how to shoot a crossbow and being my go-to source for all things related to hunting and survival.

Thank you to Cyd McDowell, Yunhee Kim, Victoria Maiolo, and Chrissy Kwasnik for being the spectacular creative team behind the photographs in this book. Thank you to my editor, Kelly Reed, and the whole team at Insight Editions for working tirelessly to make this book the very best it could be. Last, but certainly never least, thank you to all my fellow *Walking Dead* fans. I hope you enjoy reading and cooking from this book as much as I enjoyed writing it!

ABOUT THE AUTHOR

Lauren Wilson is a professional chef and cookbook author. She graduated with honors from Toronto's George Brown Chef School in 2008. Since then, she has worked in various capacities in the food world, from fine dining to cheese-mongering, online sales, catering, teaching cooking classes, and writing for print and online media. She is the author of *The Art of Eating Through the Zombie Apocalypse*, an illustrated cookbook and culinary survival guide. She lives in Brooklyn, NY.

RESOURCES

Specialty Ingredients

Sue's Acorn Flour, http://www.buyacornflour.com/

Fossil Farms, http://www.fossilfarms.com/

Specialty Meats & Gourmet, http://www.smgfoods.com/

Broken Arrow Ranch, http://www.brokenarrowranch.com/

Dehydrated, Powdered, and Freeze-dried Foods:

Augason Farms, http://www.augasonfarms.com/

Harmony House Foods, http://www.harmonyhousefoods.com/

Honeyville, http://www.honeyville.com/

The Ready Store, https://www.thereadystore.com/

PrepareWise, http://www.preparewise.com/

Food Equipment

Fermentools, https://www.fermentools.com/

Pleasant Hill Grain, http://pleasanthillgrain.com/

Cultures for Health, http://www.culturesforhealth.com/

Aqua Flex, https://www.aquaflex.net/

Survival Gear

Cabela's, http://www.cabelas.com/

REI, https://www.rei.com/

Bass Pro Shops, http://www.basspro.com/

FURTHER READING

Foraging

Elias, Thomas, and Peter Dykeman. *Edible Wild Plants: A North American Field Guide to Over 200 Natural Foods.* Sterling Publishing, 2009.

Vorass Herrera, Melany. *Front Yard Forager: Identifying, Collecting, and Cooking the 30 Most Common Urban Weeds.* Skipstone, 2013.

Gardening

Ashworth, Suzanne. *Seed to Seed: Seed Saving and Growing Techniques for Vegetable Gardeners.* Seed Savers Exchange, 2002.

Fry, Jeff. *Preparedness Gardening: How to Grow Real Sustenance and Naturally Build Soil Fertility in Troubled Times.* Kindle e-book, 2016.

Markham, Brett L. *Mini-Farming: Self-Sufficiency on 1/4 Acre.* Skyhorse Publishing, 2010.

Riotte, Louise. *Carrots Love Tomatoes: Secrets of Companion Planting for Successful Gardening.* Storey Publishing, 1998.

Hunting

Nickens, T. Edward. *Field & Stream Skills Guide: Hunting: Hunting Skills You Need.* Weldon Owen, 2012.

Rinella, Steven. *The Complete Guide to Hunting, Butchering, and Cooking Wild Game: Volume 2: Small Game and Fowl.* Speigel & Grau, 2015.

Sprouting

Wigmore, Ann. *The Sprouting Book: How to Grow and Use Sprouts to Maximize Your Health and Vitality.* Avery, 1986.

Food Preservation

Gardeners and Farmers of Terre Vivante, The. *Preserving Food Without Freezing or Canning: Traditional Techniques Using Salt, Oil, Sugar, Alcohol, Vinegar, Drying, Cold Storage, and Lactic Fermentation.* Chelsea Green Publishing, 2007.

Katz, Sandor Ellix. *The Art of Fermentation: An In-Depth Exploration of Essential Concepts and Processes from Around the World.* Chelsea Green Publishing, 2012.

Ruhlman, Michael, and Brian Polcyn. *Charcuterie: The Craft of Salting, Smoking, and Curing.* W. W. Norton & Company, 2005.

West, Kevin. *Saving the Season: A Cook's Guide to Home Canning, Pickling, and Preserving.* Knopf, 2013.

General Survival

Angier, Bradford. *How to Stay Alive in the Woods: A Complete Guide to Food, Shelter, and Self-Preservation that Makes Starvation in the Wilderness Next to Impossible.* Touchstone, 1998.

Graves, Richard. *Bushcraft: The Ultimate Guide to Survival in the Wilderness.* Skyhorse Publishing, 2013.

Mettler, John J. Jr., DVM. *Basic Butchering of Livestock & Game.* Storey Publishing, 1986.

Stewart, Creek. *Survival Hacks: Over 200 Ways to Use Everyday Items for Wilderness Survival.* Adams Media, 2016.

Wiseman, John "Lofty." *SAS Survival Handbook, Third Edition: The Ultimate Guide to Surviving Anywhere.* William Morrow Paperbacks, 2014.

Measurements Conversion Charts

Volume

US	METRIC
⅕ teaspoon	1 milliliter
1 teaspoon (tsp)	5 milliliter
1 tablespoon (tbsp)	15 milliliter
1 fluid ounce	30 milliliter
⅕ cup	50 milliliter
¼ cup	60 milliliter
⅓ cup	80 milliliter
3.4 fluid ounces	100 milliliter
½ cup	120 milliliter
⅔ cup	160 milliliter
¾ cup	180 milliliter
1 cup	240 milliliter
1 pint (2 cups)	480 milliliter
1 quart (4 cups)	.95 liter

Weight

US	METRIC
0.5 ounce	14 grams
1 ounce	28 grams
¼ pound (lb)	113 grams
⅓ pound (lb)	151 grams
½ pound (lb)	227 grams
1 pound (lb)	454 grams

Temperatures

FAHRENHEIT	CELSIUS
200°	93.3°
212°	100°
250°	121°
275°	149°
325°	165°
350°	177°
400°	205°
425°	220°
450°	233°
475°	245°
500°	260°

INSIGHT EDITIONS

PO Box 3088
San Rafael, CA 94912
www.insighteditions.com

 Find us on Facebook: www.facebook.com/InsightEditions
 Follow us on Twitter: @insighteditions

Library of Congress Cataloging-in-Publication Data available.

ISBN: 978-1-68383-078-8

Publisher: Raoul Goff
Associate Publisher: Vanessa Lopez
Art Director: Chrissy Kwasnik
Project Editor: Kelly Reed
Editorial Assistant: Hilary VandenBroek
Managing Editor: Alan Kaplan
Production Editor: Elaine Ou
Production Manager: Alix Nicholaeff

Illustrations by Sophy Tuttle

Insight Editions would like to thank Mary Johnson and Maya Meissner from the
Pat Bates Agency and the talented team behind the photos—photographer Yunhee Kim,
prop stylist Victoria Maiolo, food stylist Cyd McDowell, and assistants Robin F. Williams
and Chelsea Leigh—as well as the crew at Columbia Products in Brooklyn, NY. Thank
you to Marc Sumerak for the writing assistance.

Insight Editions, in association with Roots of Peace, will plant two trees for each tree
used in the manufacturing of this book. Roots of Peace is an internationally renowned
humanitarian organization dedicated to eradicating land mines worldwide and
converting war-torn lands into productive farms and wildlife habitats. Roots of Peace
will plant two million fruit and nut trees in Afghanistan and provide farmers there
with the skills and support necessary for sustainable land use.

Manufactured in China by Insight Editions

10 9 8 7 6 5 4

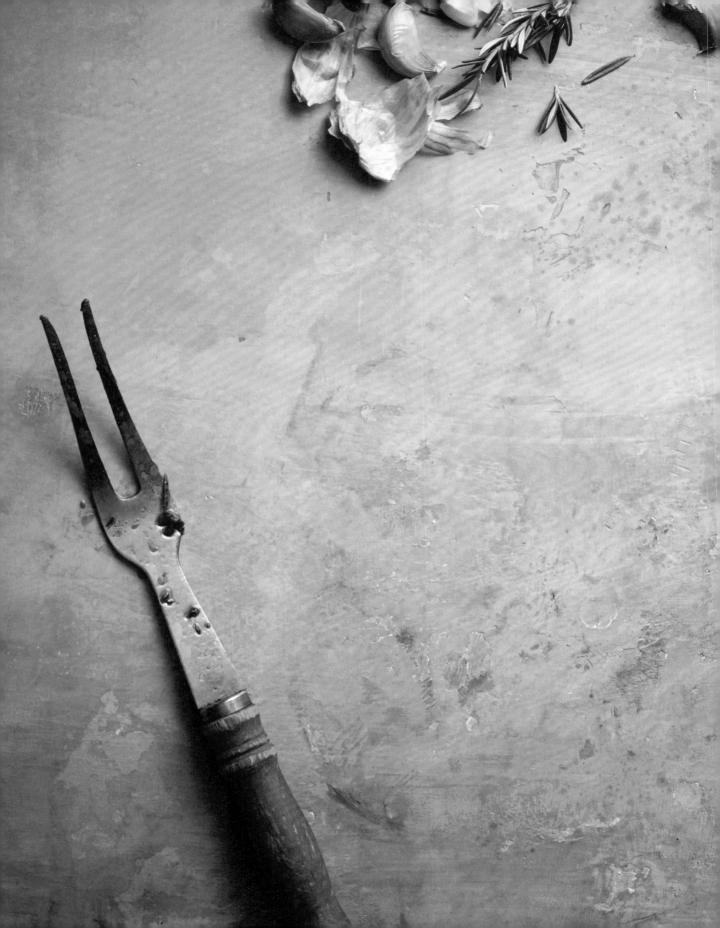